AAT

Qualifications and Credit Framework (QCF)

AQ2013
LEVEL 2 CERTIFICATE IN ACCOUNTING

(QCF)

book is to

QUESTION BANK

Control Accounts, Journals and the Banking System

2014 Edition

For assessments from September 2014

Second edition June 2014
ISBN 9781 4727 0932 5

Previous edition
ISBN 9781 4727 0346 0

British Library Cataloguing-in-Publication Data
A catalogue record for this book is available from the British Library

Published by
BPP Learning Media Ltd
BPP House
Aldine Place
London W12 8AA

www.bpp.com/learningmedia

Printed in the United Kingdom by Martins of Berwick
Sea View Works
Spittal
Berwick-Upon-Tweed
TD15 1RS

We are grateful to the AAT for permission to reproduce the sample
assessment(s). The answers to the sample assessment(s) have been
published by the AAT. All other answers have been prepared by BPP
Learning Media Ltd.

BPP
LEARNING MEDIA

CONTENTS

Introduction   v

Question and answer bank

Chapter tasks		Questions	Answers
1	Bank reconciliations	3	53
2	Introduction to control accounts	14	60
3	Preparing and reconciling control accounts	19	63
4	The journal	29	70
5	Errors and the trial balance	35	74
6	The banking system	47	82
AAT AQ2013 Sample Assessment 1		87	109
AAT AQ2013 Sample Assessment 2		123	147
BPP Practice Assessment 1 ✓		161	179
BPP Practice Assessment 2 ✓		191	211
BPP Practice Assessment 3		223	243

A NOTE ABOUT COPYRIGHT

Dear Customer

What does the little © mean and why does it matter?

Your market-leading BPP books, course materials and e-learning materials do not write and update themselves. People write them on their own behalf or as employees of an organisation that invests in this activity. Copyright law protects their livelihoods. It does so by creating rights over the use of the content.

Breach of copyright is a form of theft – as well being a criminal offence in some jurisdictions, it is potentially a serious breach of professional ethics.

With current technology, things might seem a bit hazy but, basically, without the express permission of BPP Learning Media:

- Photocopying our materials is a breach of copyright

- Scanning, ripcasting or conversion of our digital materials into different file formats, uploading them to facebook or emailing them to your friends is a breach of copyright

You can, of course, sell your books, in the form in which you have bought them – once you have finished with them. (Is this fair to your fellow students? We update for a reason.) Please note the e-products are sold on a single user licence basis: we do not supply 'unlock' codes to people who have bought them secondhand.

And what about outside the UK? BPP Learning Media strives to make our materials available at prices students can afford by local printing arrangements, pricing policies and partnerships which are clearly listed on our website. A tiny minority ignore this and indulge in criminal activity by illegally photocopying our material or supporting organisations that do. If they act illegally and unethically in one area, can you really trust them?

INTRODUCTION

This is BPP Learning Media's AAT Question Bank for Control Accounts, Journals and the Banking System. It is part of a suite of ground-breaking resources produced by BPP Learning Media for the AAT's assessments under the Qualification and Credit Framework.

The Control Accounts, Journals and the Banking System assessment will be **computer assessed**. As well as being available in the traditional paper format, this **Question Bank is available in an online environment** containing tasks similar to those you will encounter in the AAT's testing environment. BPP Learning Media believe that the best way to practise for an online assessment is in an online environment. However, if you are unable to practise in the online environment you will find that all tasks in the paper Question Bank have been written in a style that is as close as possible to the style that you will be presented with in your online assessment.

This Question Bank has been written in conjunction with the BPP Text, and has been carefully designed to enable students to practise all of the learning outcomes and assessment criteria for the units that make up Control Accounts, Journals and the Banking System. It is fully up-to-date as at June 2014 and reflects both the AAT's unit guide and the sample assessment(s) provided by the AAT.

This Question Bank contains these key features:

- Tasks corresponding to each chapter of the Text. Some tasks are designed for learning purposes, others are of assessment standard

- The AAT's AQ2013 Sample Assessments and answers for Control Accounts, Journals and the Banking System and further BPP practice assessments

The emphasis in all tasks and assessments is on the practical application of the skills acquired.

VAT

You may find tasks throughout this Question Bank that need you to calculate or be aware of a rate of VAT. This is stated at 20% in these examples and questions.

Approaching the assessment

When you sit the assessment it is very important that you follow the on screen instructions. This means you need to carefully read the instructions, both on the introduction screens and during specific tasks.

When you access the assessment you should be presented with an introductory screen with information similar to that shown below (taken from the introductory screen from one of the AAT's AQ2013 Sample Assessments for Control Accounts, Journals and the Banking System.

Each task is independent. You will not need to refer to your answers to previous tasks. Read every task carefully to make sure you understand what is required.

Where the date is relevant, it is given in the task data.

Both minus signs and brackets can be used to indicate negative numbers UNLESS task instructions say otherwise.

**You must use a full stop to indicate a decimal point.
For example, write 100.57 NOT 100,57 or 100 57**

You may use a comma to indicate a number in the thousands. But you don't have to. For example, 10000 and 10,000 are both OK.

Other indicators are not compatible with the computer-marked system.

Complete all 12 tasks

For Control Accounts, Journals and the Banking System the instructions on the introduction screen make it clear that the tasks in the assessment are set in a business situation where the following conditions (taken from the second sample assessment) apply:

- 'You are employed by the business, Gold, as a bookkeeper.

- Gold uses a manual accounting system.

- Double entry takes place in the general ledger. Individual accounts of trade receivables and trade payables are kept in the sales and purchases ledgers as subsidiary accounts.

- The cash-book and petty cash-book should be treated as part of the double entry system unless the task instructions state otherwise.

- The VAT rate is 20%.'

It is very important you read the instructions on the introductory screen and apply them in the assessment. You don't want to lose marks when you know the correct answer just because you have not entered it in the right format.

In general, the rules set out in the AAT Sample Assessments for the subject you are studying for will apply in the real assessment, but you should carefully read the information on this screen again in the real assessment, just to make sure. This screen may also confirm the VAT rate used if applicable.

A full stop is needed to indicate a decimal point. We would recommend using minus signs to indicate negative numbers and leaving out the comma signs to indicate thousands, as this results in a lower number of key strokes and less margin for error when working under

time pressure. Having said that, you can use whatever is easiest for you as long as you operate within the rules set out for your particular assessment.

You have to show competence throughout the assessment and you should therefore complete all of the tasks. Don't leave questions unanswered.

In some assessments, written or complex tasks may be human marked. In this case you are given a blank space or table to enter your answer into. You are told in the assessments which tasks these are (note: there may be none if all answers are marked by the computer).

If these involve calculations, it is a good idea to decide in advance how you are going to lay out your answers to such tasks by practising answering them on a word document, and certainly you should try all such tasks in this Question Bank and in the AAT's environment using the sample/practice assessments.

When asked to fill in tables, or gaps, never leave any blank even if you are unsure of the answer. Fill in your best estimate.

Note that for some assessments where there is a lot of scenario information or tables of data provided (eg tax tables), you may need to access these via 'pop-ups'. Instructions will be provided on how you can bring up the necessary data during the assessment.

Finally, take note of any task specific instructions once you are in the assessment. For example you may be asked to enter a date in a certain format or to enter a number to a certain number of decimal places.

Remember you can practise the BPP questions in this Question Bank in an online environment on our dedicated AAT Online page. On the same page is a link to the current AAT Sample Assessments as well.

If you have any comments about this book, please email ianblackmore@bpp.com or write to Ian Blackmore, AAT Range Manager, BPP Learning Media Ltd, BPP House, Aldine Place, London W12 8AA.

Question bank

Control Accounts, Journals and the Banking System Question bank

Chapter 1 Bank reconciliations

Task 1.1

Would each of the following transactions appear as a payment in or a payment out on a business's bank statement?

Transaction	Payment out ✓	Payment in ✓
£470.47 paid into the bank		✓
Standing order of £26.79	✓	
Cheque payment of £157.48	✓	
Interest earned on the bank balance		✓
BACS payment for wages	✓	

Task 1.2

You are given information about Newmans' receipts during the week ending 27 January. They represent payments by credit customers and receipts for sales to non-credit customers of music, instruments and CDs which were settled by cheque.

From Tunfield District Council – £594.69

From Tunshire County Orchestra £468.29

Sales of music (no VAT) – paid by cheque £478.90

From Tunfield Brass Band £1,059.72

Sales of instruments (including VAT) – paid by cheque £752.16

Sales of CDs (including VAT) – paid by cheque £256.80

Write up and total the debit side of the cash book given below:

Cash book – debit side

Date	Details	Bank £
	Bal b/f	379.22
	Tunfield DC	594.69
	Tunshire CO	468.29
	Non-credit sales	478.90
	Tunfield BB	1059.72
	Non credit sales	752.16
27 Jan	Non credit sales	256.8
		3989.78

Task 1.3

Given below is the credit side of the cash book for Newmans for the week ending 27 January.

Cash book – credit side

Date	Cheque no	Details	Bank £
27 Jan	003014	Henson Press	329.00
27 Jan	003015	Ely Instr	736.96
27 Jan	003016	Jester Press	144.67
27 Jan	003017	CD Supplies	74.54
27 Jan	003018	Jester Press	44.79
27 Jan	003019	Buser Ltd	273.48
27 Jan	SO	Rates	255.00
27 Jan	DD	Rent	500.00

Given below is the bank statement for Newmans for the week ending 27 January.

STATEMENT

first national
26 Pinehurst Place
London
EC1 2AA

NEWMANS
Account number: 20 26-33 40208134

CHEQUE ACCOUNT
Sheet 023

Date		Paid out	Pain in	Balance
20XX				
20 Jan	Balance b/f			379.22 CR
24 Jan	BGC – Tunsfield		594.69	
	BGC – Tunshire Co		468.29	
24 Jan	SO – British Elec =Standing Order	212.00		1,230.20 CR
25 Jan	BGC – Tunsfield AOS		108.51	1,338.71 CR
26 Jan	Cheque No 003014	329.00		
	Credit		478.90	1,488.61 CR
27 Jan	Cheque No 003017	74.54		
	Cheque No 003015	736.96		
	Credit		1,059.72	
	Credit		752.16	
	SO – TDC	255.00		
	DD – Halpern Properties	500.00		
	Bank interest		3.68	1,737.67 CR

Compare the two sides of the cash book from Tasks 1.2 and 1.3 to the bank statement. Note any unmatched items below and state what action you would take.

Unmatched item	Action to be taken
3.60. Bank Interest	
368 Bank Interest	
Cheque no 003016 144.67	Unpresented cheque – will appear on the bank bank reconciliation statmet
Cheque no 003018 47.75	Unpresated cheque
Cheque no 003019 273.60	Unpresated cheque

Task 1.4

Amend both sides of the cash book and find the balance on the cash book at 27 January.

Cash book – debit side

Date	Details	Bank £
	Balance b/f	379.22
27 Jan	Tunfield DC	594.69
27 Jan	Tunshire CO	468.29
27 Jan	Non-credit sales	478.90
27 Jan	Tunfield BB	1,059.72
27 Jan	Non-credit sales	752.16
27 Jan	Reinhardt plc	256.80

Cash book – credit side

Date	Cheque no	Details	Bank £
27 Jan	003014	Henson Press	329.00
27 Jan	003015	Ely Instr	736.96
27 Jan	003016	Jester Press	144.67
27 Jan	003017	CD Supplies	74.54
27 Jan	003018	Jester Press	44.79
27 Jan	003019	Buser Ltd	273.48
27 Jan	SO	Rates	255.00
27 Jan	DD	Rent	500.00

Task 1.5

Prepare the bank reconciliation statement as at 27 January.

Bank reconciliation statement as at 27 January	£	£
Balance per bank statement		
Outstanding lodgement		
Total to add		
Unpresented cheques		
Total to subtract		
Amended cash book balance		

Task 1.6

On 28 November The Flower Chain received the following bank statement as at 25 November:

High Street Bank plc
The Concourse, Badley, B72 5DG

To: The Flower Chain   Account no: 28710191   Date: 25 November

Statement of Account

Date	Details	Paid out £	Paid in £	Balance £
03 Nov	Balance b/f			9,136 C
07 Nov	Cheque 110870	6,250		2,886 C
17 Nov	Cheque 110872	2,250		636 C
21 Nov	Cheque 110865	3,670		3,034 D
	Direct Debit – Insurance Ensured	500		3,534 D
21 Nov	Bank Giro Credit – BBT Ltd		10,000	6,466 C
24 Nov	Bank Giro Credit – Petals Ltd		2,555	9,021 C
	Direct Debit – Rainbow Ltd	88		8,933 C
25 Nov	Cheque 110871	1,164		7,769 C

D = Debit C = Credit

The cash book as at 28 November is shown below.

Cash book

Date	Details	Bank £	Date		Details	Bank £
01 Nov	Balance b/f	5,466	03 Nov	110870	Roberts & Co	6,250
24 Nov	Bevan & Co	1,822	03 Nov	110871	J Jones	1,164
24 Nov	Plant Pots Ltd	7,998	06 Nov	110872	Lake Walks Ltd	2,250
			10 Nov	110873	PH Supplies	275
			17 Nov	110874	Peters & Co	76

(a) **Check the items on the bank statement against the items in the cash book.**

(b) **Update the cash book as needed.**

(c) **Total the cash book and clearly show the balance carried down at 28 November AND brought down at 29 November.**

(d) **Using the information from the cash book and bank statement, prepare a bank reconciliation statement as at 28 November.**

Bank reconciliation statement as at 28 November	£	£
Balance per bank statement		
Outstanding lodgements		
Total to add		
Unpresented cheques		
Total to subtract		
Balance as per cash book		

Task 1.7

(a) **Which TWO of the following items reconciling the cash book to the bank statement are referred to as timing differences?**

	Timing difference? ✓
Bank charges not recorded in the cash book	
Outstanding lodgements	✔
Interest charged not recorded in the cash book	
Unpresented cheques	✔

(b) Your cash book at 31 December shows a bank balance of £565 overdrawn. On comparing this with your bank statement at the same date, you discover the following:

A cheque for £57 drawn by you on 29 December has not yet been presented for payment. *not effect*

A cheque for £92 from a customer, which was paid into the bank on 24 December, has been dishonoured on 31 December. *565 + 92 = 657*

The correct bank balance at 31 December is:

	✓
£714 overdrawn	
£657 overdrawn	✔
£473 overdrawn	
£530 overdrawn	

(c) The cash book shows a bank balance of £5,675 overdrawn at 31 August. It is subsequently discovered that a standing order for £125 has been entered in the cash book twice, and that a dishonoured cheque for £450 has been debited in the cash book instead of credited. *didn't get through*

The correct bank balance should be:

	✓
£5,100 overdrawn	
£6,000 overdrawn	
£6,250 overdrawn	
£6,450 overdrawn	✔

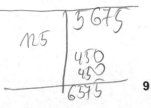

$$125 \overline{)\begin{array}{l} 5675 \\ 450 \\ 45 \\ \hline 6375 \end{array}}$$

(d) Your firm's cash book at 30 April shows a balance at the bank of £2,490. Comparison with the bank statement at the same date reveals the following differences:

£ 2490

	£
Unpresented cheques	840
Bank charges	50 —
Receipts not yet credited by the bank	470
Dishonoured cheque from customer not in cash book	140

The correct balance on the cash book at 30 April is:

	✓
£1,460	
£2,300	✓
£2,580	
£3,140	

(e) The bank statement at 31 December 20X1 shows a balance of £1,000. The cash book shows a balance of £750.

Which of the following is the most likely reason for the difference?

	✓
Receipts of £250 recorded in cash book, but not yet recorded by bank	
Bank charges of £250 shown on the bank statement, not in the cash book	
Standing orders of £250 included on bank statement, not in the cash book	
Cheques issued for £250 recorded in the cash book, but not yet gone through the bank account	

(f) Your firm's cash book at 30 April shows a balance at the bank of £3,526. Comparison with the bank statement at the same date reveals the following differences:

	£
Unpresented cheques	920
Bank interest received not in cash book	150
Uncredited lodgements	270
Dishonour of customer's cheque not in cash book	310

The correct cash book balance at 30 April is:

£ [   ]

Task 1.8

On 26 July Ottaways Ltd received the following bank statement from Ronda Bank as at 23 July.

Assume today's date is 28 July.

Ronda Bank PLC

Bank Buildings, Flitweck, FT87 1XQ

To: Ottaways Ltd   Account No 56235472   23 July

Statement of Account

Date	Detail	Paid out	Paid in	Balance	
20XX		£	£	£	
03 Jul	Balance b/f			1,855	C
03 Jul	Cheque 126459	3,283		1,428	D
03 Jul	Cheque 126460	1,209		2,637	D
03 Jul	Cheque 126461	4,221		6,858	D
04 Jul	Cheque 126464	658		7,516	D
09 Jul	Bank Giro Credit SnipSnap Co		8,845	1,329	C
11 Jul	Cheque 126462	1,117		212	C
11 Jul	Direct Debit Flit DC	500		288	D
18 Jul	Direct Debit Consol Landlords	475		763	D
20 Jul	Bank Charges	32		795	D
22 Jul	Interest for month	103		898	D
23 Jul	Paid in at Ronda Bank		5,483	4,585	C

D = Debit   C = Credit

The cash book as at 23 July is shown below.

(a) **Check the items on the bank statement against the items in the cash book.**

(b) **Using the picklist below for the details column, enter any items in the cash book as needed.**

(c) **Total the cash book and clearly show the balance carried down at 23 July and brought down at 24 July.**

(d) **Using the picklist below, complete the bank reconciliation statement as at 23 July.**

Cash book

Date	Details	Bank £	Date	Cheque number	Details	Bank £
01 Jul	Balance b/f	1,855	01 Jul	126459	Gumpley Co	3,283
20 Jul	Brimfull Ltd	5,483	01 Jul	126460	Warnes Ltd	1,209
21 Jul	Adera Ltd	2,198	01 Jul	126461	Veldt Partners	4,221
22 Jul	Mist Northern	1,004	01 Jul	126462	Pathways	1,117
	▼		02 Jul	126463	Lindstrom Co	846
	▼		02 Jul	126464	Kestrels Training	658
	▼		13 Jul	126465	HGW Ltd	3,200
	▼		13 Jul		Flit DC	500
	▼				▼	
	▼				▼	
	▼				▼	
	▼				▼	
	Total				Total	
	▼				▼	

Bank reconciliation statement as at 23 July	£	£
Balance per bank statement		
Outstanding lodgements		
Total to add		
Unpresented cheques		
Total to subtract		
Balance as per cash book		

Picklist:
Adera Ltd
Balance b/d
Balance c/d
Bank charges
Brimfull Ltd
Consol Landlords
Flit DC
Gumpley Co
HGW Ltd
Interest
Kestrels Training
Lindstrom Co
Mist Northern
Pathways
SnipSnap Co
Veldt Partners
Warnes Ltd

Chapter 2 Introduction to control accounts

Proforma p.102 Kaplan

Task 2.1

Your organisation is not registered for VAT. The balance on the sales ledger control account on 1 January was £11,689. The transactions that take place during January are summarised below:

	£
Credit sales	12,758
Sales returns	1,582
Cash received from trade receivables	11,563
Discounts allowed to trade receivables	738
Irrecoverable debt to be written off	389
Dishonoured cheque from customer	722

You are required to write up the sales ledger control account for the month of January.

14272

Sales ledger control

	£		£
Balance b/d	11689	Sales returns	1582
	12758	Bank	11363
Bank (dishonoured cheque)	722	Discounts allowed	738
		Irrecoverable debt	389
		balance c/d	10897
	25169		25169

Task 2.2

Your organisation is not registered for VAT. The opening balance on the purchases ledger control account at 1 January was £8,347. The transactions for the month of January have been summarised below:

	£
Credit purchases	9,203
Purchases returns	728
Payments to trade payables	8,837
Discounts received	382

You are required to write up the purchases ledger control account for the month of January.

9947 *pM2*

Purchases ledger control

	£		£
Purchase return	728	Balance b/d	8347
Payments to trade payables	8837	Purchases	9203
Discount received	382		
Balac c/d	7603		
	17550		17550

Task 2.3

This is a summary of transactions with credit suppliers during June.

	£
Balance of trade payables at 1 June	85,299
Goods bought on credit – gross	39,300
Payments made to credit suppliers	33,106
Discounts received	1,000
Goods returned to credit suppliers – gross	275

Prepare a purchases ledger control account from the details shown above. Show clearly the balance carried down at 30 June AND brought down at 1 July.

Purchases ledger control

Date	Details	Amount £	Date	Details	Amount £
	Bank	33106			85299 39300

Task 2.4

(a) The sales ledger control account at 1 May had a balance of £31,475. During May, gross sales of £125,000 were made on credit. Receipts from trade receivables amounted to £122,500 and settlement discounts of £550 were allowed. Credit notes of £1,300 gross were issued to customers.

The closing balance at 31 May is:

	✓
£32,125	
£33,975	
£34,725	
£33,225	

(b) Your purchases ledger control account has a balance at 1 October of £34,500 credit. During October, gross credit purchases were £78,400, gross cash purchases were £2,400 and payments made to suppliers, excluding cash purchases, and after deducting settlement discounts of £1,200, were £68,900. Gross purchases returns were £4,700.

The closing balance was:

	✓
£38,100	
£40,500	
£47,500	
£49,900	

Task 2.5

Assuming they all include VAT where relevant, identify the double entry for the following transactions.

	Bank £	SLCA £	PLCA £	VAT £	Purchases £	Sales returns £	Discounts received £	Discounts allowed £
	DR/CR	DR/CR	DR/CR	DR/CR	DR/CR	DR/CR	DR/CR	DR/CR
Gross credit purchases £3,390								
Gross credit sales returns £1,860								
Payments to credit suppliers £4,590								
Receipts from credit customers £5,480								
Discounts allowed £400								
Discounts received £200								

Task 2.6

A credit customer, B B Brand Ltd, has ceased trading, owing Kitchen Kuts £1,560 plus VAT.

Record the journal entries needed in the general ledger to write off the net amount and the VAT.

Account name	Amount £	Debit ✓	Credit ✓

....

Chapter 3 Preparing and reconciling control accounts

Task 3.1

When reconciling sales ledger and purchases ledger control accounts to the list of balances from the subsidiary ledgers, would the following errors affect the relevant control account, the list of balances or both?

	Control account ✓	List of balances ✓	Both ✓
Invoice entered into the sales day book as £980 instead of £890			
Purchases day book overcast by £1,000			
Discounts allowed of £20 not entered into the cash book (debit side)			
An invoice taken as £340 instead of £440 when being posted to the customer's account			
Incorrect balancing of a subsidiary ledger account			
A purchases return not entered into the purchases returns day book			

Task 3.2

James has just completed his first month of trading. James makes sales on credit to four customers and the transactions during his second month of trading were as follows:

Gross sales	£
To H Simms	2,000
To P Good	2,700
To K Mitchell	1,100
To C Brown	3,800

Receipts	£
From H Simms	2,400
From P Good	3,600
From K Mitchell	1,100
From C Brown	4,800

You are required to:

(a) **Show these transactions in total in the sales ledger control account and in detail in the individual sales ledger accounts. Each of the accounts shows, where appropriate, the opening balance at the start of the second month.**

(b) **Balance the sales ledger control account and the individual sales ledger accounts.**

(c) **Reconcile the list of sales ledger balances to the balance on the control account.**

Sales ledger control

	£		£
Balance b/f	5,000		

Sales ledger

H Simms

	£		£
Balance b/f	900		

P Good

	£		£
Balance b/f	1,600		

K Mitchell

	£		£

C Brown

	£		£
Balance b/f	2,500		

Reconciliation of sales ledger balances with control account balance

	£
H Simms	
P Good	
K Mitchell	
C Brown	
Sales ledger control account	

Task 3.3

James also buys goods on credit from three suppliers. The transactions with these suppliers in month two are summarised below:

	£
Gross purchases:	
From J Peters	1,600
From T Sands	2,500
From L Farmer	3,200
Payments:	
To J Peters	1,700
To T Sands	3,200
To L Farmer	3,000

You are required to:

(a) Show these transactions in total in the purchases ledger control account and in detail in the individual purchases ledger accounts given. Each of the accounts given shows the opening balance at the start of month two.

(b) Balance the purchases ledger control account and the individual purchases ledger accounts.

(c) Reconcile the list of purchases ledger balances to the balance on the control account.

Purchases ledger control

	£		£
		Balance b/f	2,700

Purchases ledger

J Peters

	£		£
		Balance b/f	300

T Sands

	£		£
		Balance b/f	1,700

L Farmer

	£		£
		Balance b/f	700

Reconciliation of purchases ledger balances with control account balance

	£
J Peters	
T Sands	
L Farmer	
Purchases ledger control account	

Task 3.4

The balance on a business's sales ledger control account at 30 June was £13,452. However the list of balances in the sales ledger totalled £12,614. The difference was investigated and the following errors were discovered:

(i)   The sales returns day book was undercast by £100.

(ii) A payment from one trade receivable had been correctly entered into the cash book as £350 but had been entered into the sales ledger as £530.

(iii) An irrecoverable debt of £200 had been written off in the sales ledger but had not been entered into the general ledger accounts.

(iv) A balance of £358 due from one trade receivable had been omitted from the list of sales ledger balances.

You are required to write up the corrected sales ledger control account and to reconcile this to the corrected list of sales ledger balances.

Sales ledger control

	£		£

	£
Sales ledger list of balances	
Error	
Error	
Amended list of balances	
Amended control account balance	

Task 3.5

The balance on an organisation's purchases ledger control account at 30 June was £26,677 whereas the total of the list of purchases ledger balances was £27,469. The following errors were discovered:

(i)   One total in the purchases day book had been undercast by £1,000.

(ii) A discount received from a supplier of £64 had not been posted to his account in the purchases ledger.

(iii) A debit balance of £120 had been included in the list of purchases ledger balances as a credit balance.

(iv) Discounts received of £256 were credited to both the discounts received account and to the purchases ledger control account.

You are required to correct the purchases ledger control account and to reconcile the corrected balance to the corrected list of purchases ledger balances.

Purchases ledger control

	£		£

	£
Purchases ledger list of balances	
Error	
Error	
Error	
Amended list of balances	
Amended control account balance	

Task 3.6

This is a summary of your business's transactions with credit customers during November.

	£
Balance of trade receivables at 1 November	48,125
Goods sold on credit (gross value)	37,008
Money received from credit customers	28,327
Discounts allowed	240
Goods returned by customers (gross value)	2,316

(a) **Prepare a sales ledger control account from the details shown above. Show clearly the balance carried down at 30 November AND brought down at 1 December.**

Sales ledger control

Date	Details	Amount £	Date	Details	Amount £

The following balances were in the sales ledger on 1 December:

	£
J Hicks Ltd	3,298
Parks and Gardens	4,109
Greener Grass	18,250
TTL Ltd	18,106
Reeves and Wright	10,400

(b) **Reconcile the balances shown above with the sales ledger control account balance you have calculated in part (a).**

	£
Sales ledger control account balance as at 1 December	
Total of sales ledger accounts as at 1 December	
Difference	

(c) **Because of an error in the sales ledger, there is a difference. What might have caused the difference? Tick TWO reasons only.**

	✓
VAT has been overstated on an invoice.	
VAT has been understated on an invoice.	
A sales invoice has been entered in the sales ledger twice.	
A sales credit note has been entered in the sales ledger twice.	
A receipt from a customer has been omitted from the sales ledger.	
A receipt from a customer has been entered in the sales ledger twice.	

Task 3.7

A business has the following transactions in one week.

	£
Credit purchases (at list price)	4,500
Sales on credit (at list price)	6,000
Purchase of a van (at list price)	10,460
Entertaining (no VAT)	360
Purchase of a car (no VAT)	8,600

A settlement discount of £300 is available on the sales. All figures are given exclusive of VAT at 20%.

If the balance on the VAT account was £2,165 credit at the beginning of the week, what is the balance at the end of the week?

£	

Task 3.8

The following transactions take place during a three month period:

	£
Sales on credit including VAT at 20%	106,800.00
Sale of assets owned for several years including VAT at 20%	20,100.00
Purchases on credit including VAT at 20%	57,810.00
Credit notes issued including VAT at 20%	2,820.00
VAT incurred on cash expenses	271.50

The amount payable to HMRC for the quarter will be

£	

Task 3.9

At the end of the last VAT period, the VAT account for Fast Fashions showed that a refund was due from HM Revenue & Customs.

(a) **State ONE reason that would cause a refund to be due to Fast Fashions.**

Sales in June totalled £129,240, all including VAT.

(b) **What is the amount of output VAT on sales?**

£

Task 3.10

(a) A supplier sends you a statement showing a balance outstanding of £14,350. Your own records show a balance outstanding of £14,500.

The reason for this difference could be that

	✓
The supplier sent an invoice for £150 which you have not yet received	
The supplier has allowed you £150 settlement discount which you had not entered in your ledger	
You have paid the supplier £150 which he has not yet accounted for	
You have returned goods worth £150 which the supplier has not yet accounted for	

(b) An invoice for £69 has been recorded in the sales day book as £96.

When the sales ledger reconciliation is prepared, adjustments will be required to:

	✓
The control account only	
The list of balances only	
Both the control account and the list of balances	

(c) The total of the balances on the individual suppliers' accounts in Arnold's purchases ledger is £81,649. The balance on the purchases ledger control account is £76,961. He has discovered that an invoice for £4,688 has been posted twice to the correct supplier's account and that payments totalling £1,606 which he made by standing order have been omitted from his records.

The corrected balance for trade payables is

£	

Task 3.11

(a) You have been handed an aged receivable analysis which shows a total balance of £109,456.

This amount should reconcile with which TWO of the following?

	✓
The balance on the bank statement	
The balance on the sales ledger control account	
The balance on the purchases ledger control account	
The total of all the purchases ledger balances	
The total of all the sales ledger balances	

(b) **Complete the following sentence:**

The aged receivable analysis shows:

	✓
How much is owed to suppliers at any point	
Over how many months the outstanding balance owed by each individual credit customer has built up	
The total purchases over the year to date to each credit supplier	

Chapter 4 The journal

Task 4.1

Peter Knight is one of the employees at Short Furniture and has a gross weekly wage of £440.00. For this week his income tax payable through the PAYE system is £77.76. The employees' NIC for the week is £43.18 and 5% of his gross wage is deducted each week as a pension contribution. The employer's NIC for the week is £49.35.

(a) **Calculate Peter's net wage for the week.**

£	

(b) **What payments and to whom should Short Furniture make in regard to Peter's wages for this week?**

£		should be paid to	
£		should be paid to	
£		should be paid to	

(c) **Show how all of the elements of Peter's weekly wage would be entered into the accounting records by writing up the ledger accounts given.**

Wages expense

		£		£

Wages control

		£		£

HMRC

		£		£

Pension payable

	£		£

Bank

	£		£

Task 4.2

An organisation has started a new business and a new set of accounts is to be opened. The opening balances for the new business are as follows:

	£
Capital	10,000
Furniture and fittings	15,315
Sales	127,318
Motor vehicles	20,109
Cash at bank	15,000
Purchases	86,120
Purchases returns	750
Purchases ledger control	37,238
Sales ledger control	53,259
Loan from bank	7,000
Motor expenses	1,213
VAT (owed to HM Revenue and Customs)	8,710

Prepare a journal to enter these opening balances into the accounts.

Journal

Account name	Debit £	Credit £
Totals		

Task 4.3

A credit customer, ABC Ltd, has ceased trading, owing your firm £240 plus VAT.

Prepare a journal to write off the net amount and VAT in the general ledger.

Journal

Account name	Amount £	Debit ✓	Credit ✓

Task 4.4

You have the following information for your business, First Fashions:

(a) £50 has been debited to the discounts received account instead of the discounts allowed account.

(b) A payment of £200 for office expenses has been credited to the bank deposit account instead of the bank current account.

(c) A credit customer, Kit & Company, has ceased trading, owing First Fashions £2,800 plus VAT. The net amount and VAT must be written off in the general ledger.

Record the journal entries needed in the general ledger to deal with this information.

Journal

Account names	Amount £	Debit ✓	Credit ✓

Task 4.5

A credit customer, Arco and Co, has ceased trading, owing your business £2,370 plus VAT.

Record the journal entries needed in the general ledger to write off the net amount and the VAT.

Account name	Amount £	Debit ✓	Credit ✓

Task 4.6

A new business has already started to trade, though it is not yet registered for VAT, and now wishes to open up its first set of accounts. You are handed the following information:

It has £1,000 in the bank, petty cash of £200 and trade receivables of £7,700. It owes the bank for a loan of £9,000 and started with cash from its owner of £500. It has made sales so far of £15,250 and purchases of £6,230, for which it still owes one supplier £3,400. Expenses paid to date have been £7,020, and a van was bought for cash of £6,000.

Record the journal entries needed in the accounts in the general ledger of the business to deal with the opening entries.

Account name	Amount £	Debit ✓	Credit ✓
Journal to record the opening entries of new business			

Task 4.7

Kitchen Kuts has started a new business, Kitchen Capers, and a new set of accounts is to be opened. A partially completed journal to record the opening entries is shown below.

Record the journal entries needed in the accounts in the general ledger of Kitchen Capers to deal with the opening entries.

Account name	Amount £	Debit ✓	Credit ✓
Cash	150		
Cash at bank	12,350		
Capital	23,456		
Fixtures and Fittings	2,100		
Insurance	825		
Loan from bank	10,000		
Miscellaneous expenses	218		
Motor vehicle	15,650		
Office expenses	613		
Rent and rates	1,550		
Journal to record the opening entries of new business			

Chapter 5 Errors and the trial balance

Task 5.1

A business extracts a trial balance in which the debit column totals £452,409 and the credit column totals £463,490.

What will be the balance on the suspense account?

Account name	Amount £	Debit ✓	Credit ✓
Suspense			

Task 5.2

A business used a suspense account with a credit balance of £124 to balance its initial trial balance.

Correction of which ONE of the following errors will clear the suspense account?

Error	✓
A credit note from a supplier with a net amount of £124 was not entered in the purchases ledger	
Discounts allowed of £124 were only posted to the discounts allowed account	
A cash purchase for £124 was not entered in the purchases account	
An irrecoverable debt write-off of £124 was not entered in the subsidiary ledger	

Task 5.3

Given below are two ledger accounts.

Examine them carefully and then re-write them correcting any errors that have been made (you may assume that the balance brought forward on the VAT account is correct).

Sales ledger control

	£		£
Sales	15,899	Balance b/f	1,683
Discounts allowed	900	Bank	14,228
Sales returns	1,467	Irrecoverable debts written off	245
		Balance c/d	2,110
	18,266		18,266

VAT

	£		£
Sales	2,368	Balance b/f	2,576
Purchase returns	115	Purchases	1,985
Balance c/d	2,078		
	4,561		18,266

Sales ledger control

Details	£	Details	£

VAT

Details	£	Details	£

Task 5.4

The trial balance of Harry Parker & Co has been prepared by the bookkeeper and the total of the debit balances is £427,365 while the total of the credit balances is £431,737. The difference was dealt with by setting up a suspense account and then the ledger accounts were investigated to try to find the causes of the difference. The following errors and omissions were found:

(i) The total of the sales day book was undercast by £1,000.

(ii) The balance on the electricity account of £1,642 had been completely omitted from the trial balance.

(iii) Discounts allowed of £865 had been entered on the wrong side of the discounts allowed account.

(iv) Receipts from trade receivables of £480 had been entered into the accounts as £840.

(v) A discount received of £120 had been completely omitted from the cash book.

You are required to:

(a) **Draft journal entries to correct each of these errors or omissions.**

Journal entries

		Account	£	£
(i)	Debit	Suspense		1000
	Credit	Sales day book	1000	
(ii)	Debit	Electricity	1,642	
	Credit	Suspense		1,642
(iii)	Debit	Discount allowed	30	
	Credit	Suspense		730
	Debit			
	Credit			
(iv)	Debit			
	Credit			
(v)	Debit			12
	Credit		1	12

(b) **Write up the suspense account showing clearly the opening balance and how the suspense account is cleared after correction of each of the errors.**

Suspense

Details	£	Details	£

Task 5.5

After extracting an initial trial balance a business finds it has a debit balance of £118 in the suspense account. You have the following information.

(a) Sales of £500 have been credited to the sales returns account.

(b) Entries to record a bank payment of £125 for office expenses have been reversed.

(c) A bank payment of £299 for purchases (no VAT) has been entered correctly in the purchases column of the cash book but as £29 in the total column.

(d) Discounts allowed of £388 were only posted to the sales ledger control account in the general ledger.

Record the journal entries needed in the general ledger to (i) reverse incorrect entries and (ii) record the transactions correctly.

The journal

Account names	Debit £	Credit £
(a)		
(b)		
(c)		
(d)		

Task 5.6

On 30 June, a suspense account of a business that is not registered for VAT has a credit balance of £720.

On 1 July, the following errors were discovered:

(i)   A bank payment of £225 has been omitted from the rent and rates account.

(ii) An irrecoverable debt expense of £945 has been credited correctly to the sales ledger control account, but debited to both the irrecoverable debt account and the sales account.

(a) **Enter the opening balance in the suspense account below.**

(b) **Make the necessary entries to clear the suspense account.**

Suspense

Date	Details	Amount £	Date	Details	Amount £

Task 5.7

(a) When posting an invoice received for building maintenance, £980 was entered on the building maintenance expense account instead of the correct amount of £890.

What correction should be made to the building maintenance expenses account?

	✓
Debit £90	
Credit £90	
Debit £1,780	
Credit £1,780	

(b) A business receives an invoice from a supplier for £2,800 which is mislaid before any entry has been made, resulting in the transaction being omitted from the books entirely.

This is an

	✓
Error of transposition	
Error of omission	
Error of principle	
Error of commission	

(c) **An error of commission is one where**

	✓
A transaction has not been recorded	
One side of a transaction has been recorded in the wrong account, and that account is of a different class to the correct account	
One side of a transaction has been recorded in the wrong account, and that account is of the same class as the correct account	
A transaction has been recorded using the wrong amount	

(d) **Which ONE of the following is an error of principle?**

	✓
A gas bill credited to the gas account and debited to the bank account	
The purchase of a non-current asset credited to the asset account and debited to the supplier's account	
The purchase of a non-current asset debited to the purchases account and credited to the supplier's account	
The payment of wages debited and credited to the correct accounts, but using the wrong amount	

(e) **Where a transaction is entered into the correct ledger accounts, but the wrong amount is used, the error is known as an error of**

	✓
Omission	
Original entry	
Commission	
Principle	

(f) When a trial balance was prepared, two ledger accounts were omitted:

Discounts received	£6,150
Discounts allowed	£7,500

A suspense account was opened.

What was the balance on the suspense account?

	✓
Debit £1,350	
Credit £1,350	
Debit £13,650	
Credit £13,650	

(g) **If a purchases return of £48 has been wrongly posted to the debit of the sales returns account, but has been correctly entered in the purchases ledger control account, the total of the trial balance would show**

	✓
The credit side to be £48 more than the debit side	
The debit side to be £48 more than the credit side	
The credit side to be £96 more than the debit side	
The debit side to be £96 more than the credit side	

(h) **Indicate whether preparing a trial balance will reveal the following errors.**

	Yes	No
Omitting both entries for a transaction		
Posting the debit entry for an invoice to an incorrect expense account		
Omitting the debit entry for a transaction		
Posting the debit entry for a transaction as a credit entry		

Task 5.8

Show which of the errors below are, or are not, disclosed by the trial balance.

Error in the general ledger	Error disclosed by the trial balance ✓	Error NOT disclosed by the trial balance ✓
Recording a bank receipt of a cash sale on the debit side of the cash sales account		
Entering an insurance expense in the administration expenses account		
Entering the discounts received account balance on the debit side of the trial balance		
Miscasting the total column of one page of the sales returns day book		
Failing to write up a dishonoured cheque in the cash book		
Recording discount allowed of £15 as £150 in the cash book		

Task 5.9

Your organisation's trial balance included a suspense account. All the bookkeeping errors have now been traced and the journal entries shown below have been recorded.

Journal entries

Account name	Debit £	Credit £
Motor vehicles	4,300	
Machinery		4,300
Suspense	750	
Sales ledger control		750
Discounts allowed	209	
Suspense		209

Post the journal entries to the general ledger accounts Dates are not required but you must complete the 'details' columns accurately.

Discounts allowed

Details	Amount £	Details	Amount £

Machinery

Details	Amount £	Details	Amount £

Motor vehicles

Details	Amount £	Details	Amount £

Sales ledger control

Details	Amount £	Details	Amount £

Suspense

Details	Amount £	Details	Amount £
		Balance b/f	541

Task 5.10

Your business extracted an initial trial balance which did not balance, and a suspense account with a debit balance of £6,290 was opened. Journal entries were subsequently prepared to correct the errors that had been found, and clear the suspense account. The list of balances in the initial trial balance, and the journal entries to correct the errors, are shown below.

Journal entries

Account name	Debit £	Credit £
Sales ledger control	2,875	
Suspense		2,875
Sales ledger control	2,875	
Suspense		2,875

Account name	Debit £	Credit £
Heat and light		5,172
Suspense	5,172	
Heat and light	5,712	
Suspense		5,712

Taking into account the journal entries, which will clear the suspense account, redraft the trial balance by placing the figures in the debit or credit column.

	Balances extracted on 30 June £	Balances at 1 July	
		Debit £	Credit £
Machinery	82,885		
Computer equipment	41,640		
Insurance	17,520		
Bank (overdraft)	13,252		
Petty cash	240		
Sales ledger control	241,500		
Purchases ledger control	134,686		
VAT (owing to HM Revenue and Customs)	19,920		
Capital	44,826		
Sales	525,092		
Purchases	269,400		
Purchases returns	16,272		
Wages	61,680		
Maintenance expenses	3,283		
Stationery	8,049		
Rent and rates	3,466		
Heat and light	5,172		
Telephone	7,596		
Marketing expenses	5,327		
Totals			

Task 5.11

Kitchen Kuts' initial trial balance includes a suspense account with a balance of £100.

The error has been traced to the sales returns day book shown below.

Sales returns day book

Date 20XX	Details	Credit note number	Total £	VAT £	Net £
30 June	Barber Bates Ltd	367	720	120	600
30 June	GTK Ltd	368	4,320	720	3,600
30 June	Peer Prints	369	960	160	800
	Totals		6,000	1,100	5,000

(a) **Identify the error and record the journal entries needed in the general ledger to**

   (i) **Remove the incorrect entry**

Account name	Amount £	Debit ✓	Credit ✓

   (ii) **Record the correct entry**

Account name	Amount £	Debit ✓	Credit ✓

   (iii) **Remove the suspense account balance**

Account name	Amount £	Debit ✓	Credit ✓

An entry to record a bank payment of £350 for heat and light has been reversed.

(b) **Record the journal entries needed in the general ledger to**

   (i) **Remove the incorrect entries**

Account name	Amount £	Debit ✓	Credit ✓

(ii) **Record the correct entries**

Account name	Amount £	Debit ✓	Credit ✓

Chapter 6 The banking system

Task 6.1

Given below are four cheques received by Southfield Electrical today, 9 January 20X6.

Check each one thoroughly and make a note in the table provided of any errors or problems that you encounter.

	Comments
Cheque from B B Berry Ltd	
Cheque from Q Q Stores	
Cheque from Dagwell Enterprises	
Cheque from Weller Enterprises	

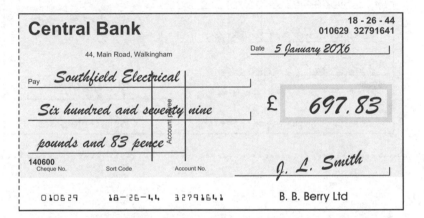

Central Bank

18 - 26 - 44
010629 32791641

44, Main Road, Walkingham

Date *5 January 20X6*

Pay *Southfield Electrical*

Six hundred and seventy nine

pounds and 83 pence

£ *697.83*

140600
Cheque No.   Sort Code   Account No.

J. L. Smith

010629   18-26-44   32791641

B. B. Berry Ltd

Northern Bank

22 - 44 - 16
10128 12976844

High Street, Drenchley

Date *7 January 20X6*

Pay *Southfield Electrical*

Two hundred and twenty eight

pounds and 60 pence

£ *228.60*

140600
Cheque No.   Sort Code   Account No.

10128   22-44-16   12976844

Q Q Stores

First Western

30 - 11 - 46
001276 43216900

High Street, Benham

Date *2 January 20X6*

Pay *Southfield Electronics*

Two hundred and forty three

Pounds only

£ *243.00*

J. Dagwell

140600
Cheque No.   Sort Code   Account No.

001276   30—11—46   43216900

Dagwell Ent.

Great National Bank

14 - 23 - 18
006411 32714986

25/27 Main Road, Benham

Date *6 January 20X5*

Pay *Southfield Electrical*

Nine hundred and eighty five

pounds and 73 pence only

£ *985.73*

T. Johnson

140600
Cheque No.   Sort Code   Account No.

006411   14—23—18   32714986

Weller Enterprises

Task 6.2

Your firm, Parker Paints, has received the following BACS remittance advice:

BACS Remittance Advice

To: Parker Paints   From: Handyman Tools Ltd

Your invoice number 1214 dated 15 October for £2,350 has been paid by BACS credit transfer and will arrive in your bank account on 1 December.

(a) **What is the earliest date these funds will be available to Parker Paints?**

(b) **Give ONE advantage to Parker Paints of being paid in this way.**

BPP
LEARNING MEDIA

Task 6.3

Complete the following statements by inserting the relevant banking terms.

(a) A [＿＿＿＿＿＿＿] would be set up to repay a bank loan in equal monthly instalments.

(b) A [＿＿＿＿＿＿＿] would be set up to make the minimum payment on a credit card by variable amounts each month.

(c) A bank [＿＿＿＿＿＿＿] would be arranged when short-term borrowing is needed.

Task 6.4

Which TWO of the documents below are banking documents that must be retained?

	✓
Statements from suppliers	
Remittance advice notes	
Orders from customers	
Direct debit agreements	
Credit notes from suppliers	
Cheque counterfoils	
Invoices to customers	

Task 6.5

Which TWO of the following items should be checked when a cheque is accepted as payment from customers?

	✓
Funds are available in customer's account	
Issue number	
Words and figures match	
Security number	
Expiry date	
Date is not in the future	

Task 6.6

An organisation that only has deposits from savers with which to make loans secured by mortgages on residential property is

	✓
A bank	
A building society	

Task 6.7

Given below is a completed cheque.

Who is the drawee?	
Who is the payee?	
Who is the drawer?	

first national

20 - 26 - 33
003014 40268134

26 Pinehurst Place, London EC1 2AA

Date *9 January 20XX*

Pay *J Peterson*

Twenty pounds only

Account payee

£ *20.00*

140600
Cheque No.   Sort Code   Account No.

F. Ronald

003014   20−26−33   40268134

F. Ronald

Answer bank

Answer bank

Control Accounts, Journals and the Banking System
Answer bank

Chapter 1

Task 1.1

Transaction	Payment out ✓	Payment in ✓
£470.47 paid into the bank		✓
Standing order of £26.79	✓	
Cheque payment of £157.48	✓	
Interest earned on the bank balance		✓
BACS payment for wages	✓	

Task 1.2

Cash book – debit side

Date	Details	Bank £
	Bal b/f	379.22
27 Jan	Tunfield DC	594.69
27 Jan	Tunshire CO	468.29
27 Jan	Non-credit sales	478.90
27 Jan	Tunfield BB	1,059.72
27 Jan	Non-credit sales	752.16
27 Jan	Non-credit sales	256.80
		3,989.78

Task 1.3

Unmatched item	Action to be taken
Bank Giro Credit Tunfield AOS	This must be checked to any supporting documentation such as any remittance advice from Tunfield AOS or the original invoice – when it has been checked the amount should be entered into the cash book
Standing order to British Elec	The standing order schedule should be checked to ensure that this is correct and it should then be entered into the cash book
Bank interest received	This should be entered into the cash book
Sales of CDs	The £256.80 cash sales of CDs settled by cheque do not appear on the bank statement. This is an outstanding lodgement that will appear in the bank reconciliation statement
Cheque number 003016	Unpresented cheque – will appear in the bank reconciliation statement
Cheque number 003018	Unpresented cheque – will appear in the bank reconciliation statement
Cheque number 003019	Unpresented cheque – will appear in the bank reconciliation statement

Handwritten annotations in left margin:
- 212. / 108.51
- 212
- 3.68
- 256.8 cash book debit
- cash book credit 144.67
- 44.79
- 273.4

Task 1.4

Cash book – debit side

Date	Details	Bank £
	Balance b/f	379.22
27 Jan	Tunfield DC	594.69✓
27 Jan	Tunshire CO	468.29✓
27 Jan	Non-credit sales	478.90✓
27 Jan	Tunfield BB	1,059.72✓
27 Jan	Non-credit sales	752.16✓
27 Jan	Reinhardt plc	256.80
27 Jan	Bank interest	3.68
27 Jan	Tunfield AOS	108.51
		4,101.97

Cash book – credit side

Date	Cheque no.	Details	Bank £
27 Jan	003014	Henson Press	329.00✓
27 Jan	003015	Ely Instr	736.96✓
27 Jan	003016	Jester Press	144.67
27 Jan	003017	CD Supplies	74.54✓
27 Jan	003018	Jester Press	44.79
27 Jan	003019	Buser Ltd	273.48
27 Jan	SO	Rates	255.00✓
27 Jan	DD	Rent	500.00✓
27 Jan	SO	British Elec	212.00✓
27 Jan		Balance c/d	1,531.53
			4,101.97

Task 1.5

Bank reconciliation statement as at 27 January	£	£
Balance per bank statement		1,737.67
Outstanding lodgement		
Reinhardt plc	256.80	
Total to add		256.80
Unpresented cheques		
003016	144.67	
003018	44.79	
003019	273.48	
Total to subtract		462.94
Amended cash book balance		1,531.53

Task 1.6

£ 10603

Cash book

Date	Details	Bank £	Date	Cheque no.	Details	Bank £
01 Nov	Balance b/f	5,466	03 Nov	110870	Roberts & Co	6,250
24 Nov	Bevan & Co	1,822	03 Nov	110871	J Jones	1,164
24 Nov	Plant Pots Ltd	7,998	06 Nov	110872	Lake Walks Ltd	2,250
21 Nov	BBT Ltd	10,000	10 Nov	110873	PH Supplies	275
24 Nov	Petals Ltd	2,555	17 Nov	110874	Peters & Co	76
			21 Nov	DD	Insurance Ensured	500
			24 Nov	DD	Rainbow Ltd	88
			28 Nov		Balance c/d	17,238
		27,841				27,841
29 Nov	Balance b/d	17,238				

Note: Cheque number 110865 on the bank statement: the first cheque in the cash book in November is number 110870. As the difference between the opening balances on the bank statement and in the cash book is for the amount of this cheque (£3,670) it is reasonable to assume that cheque 110865 was entered in the cash book in a previous month and would have been a reconciling item in the bank reconciliation in the previous month. This cheque should be ticked to the October bank reconciliation.

Bank reconciliation statement as at 28 November	£	£
Balance per bank statement: *Closing*		7,769
Outstanding lodgements		
Bevan & Co *Debit*	1,822	
Plant Pots Ltd	7,998	
Total to add		9,820
Unpresented cheques		
PH Supplies *Credit*	275	
Peters & Co	76	
Total to subtract		351
Balance as per cash book		17,238

Task 1.7

(a) The correct answers are: Outstanding lodgements and Unpresented cheques. The other two items are amended in the cash book.

(b) The correct answer is: £657 overdrawn

Working

£(565) o/d + £92 dishonoured cheque = £(657) o/d

(c) The correct answer is: £6,450 overdrawn

Workings

	£	£
Balance b/f		5,675
Reversal – Standing order entered twice	125	
Reversal – Dishonoured cheque entered in error as a debit		450
Correction – Dishonoured cheque		450
Balance c/d (overdraft)	6,450	
	6,575	6,575

[handwritten annotation: correct]

(d) The correct answer is: £2,300

Workings

	£
Cash book balance	2,490
Adjustment re charges	(50)
Adjustment re dishonoured cheque from customer	(140)
	2,300

(e) The correct answer is: Cheques issued for £250 recorded in the cash book, but not yet gone through the bank account

All the other options would have the bank account £250 less than the cash book.

(f) The correct answer is: £3,366

Workings

	£
Balance per cash book	3,526
Plus: bank interest received	150
Less: dishonoured cheque	(310)
Amended cash book balance	3,366

Task 1.8

Cash book

Date	Details	Bank £	Date	Cheque number	Details	Bank £
01 Jul	Balance b/f	1,855	01 Jul	126459	Gumpley Co	3,283
20 Jul	Brimfull Ltd	5,483	01 Jul	126460	Warnes Ltd	1,209
21 Jul	Adera Ltd	2,198	01 Jul	126461	Veldt Partners	4,221
22 Jul	Mist Northern	1,004	01 Jul	126462	Pathways	1,117
9 Jul	Snip Snap Co	8,845	02 Jul	126463	Lindstrom Co	846
			02 Jul	126464	Kestrels Training	658
			13 Jul	126465	HGW Ltd	3,200
			13 Jul		Flit DC	500
			18 Jul		Consol Landlords	475
			20 Jul		Bank charges	32
			22 Jul		Interest	103
			23 Jul		Balance c/d	3,741
	Total	19,385			Total	19,385
24 Jul	Balance b/d	3,741				

Bank reconciliation statement as at 23 July	£	£
Balance per bank statement		4,585
Outstanding lodgements		
Adera Ltd	2,198	
Mist Northern	1,004	
Total to add		3,202
Unpresented cheques		
Lindstrom Co	846	
HGW Ltd	3,200	
Total to subtract		4,046
Balance as per cash book		3,741

Chapter 2

Task 2.1

Sales ledger control

	£		£
Balance b/f	11,689	Sales returns	1,582
Sales	12,758	Bank	11,563
Bank (dishonoured cheque)	722	Discounts allowed	738
		Irrecoverable debt written off	389
		Balance c/d	10,897
	25,169		25,169

Task 2.2

Purchases ledger control

	£		£
Purchases returns	728	Balance b/f	8,347
Bank	8,837	Purchases	9,203
Discounts received	382		
Balance c/d	7,603		
	17,550		17,550

Task 2.3

Purchases ledger control

Date	Details	Amount £	Date	Details	Amount £
30 June	Bank	33,106	1 June	Balance b/f	85,299
30 June	Discounts received	1,000	30 June	Purchases	39,300
30 June	Purchases returns	275			
30 June	Balance c/d	90,218			
		124,599			124,599
			1 July	Balance b/d	90,218

Task 2.4

(a) The correct answer is: £32,125

Working

£31,475 + £125,000 – £122,500 – £550 – £1,300 = £32,125 debit

(b) The correct answer is: £38,100

Working

	£
Opening balance	34,500
Credit purchases	78,400
Discounts received	(1,200)
Payments	(68,900)
Purchases returns	(4,700)
	38,100

....

Task 2.5

	Bank	SLCA £	PLCA £	VAT £	Purchases £	Sales returns £	Discounts received £	Discounts allowed £
	DR/CR	DR/CR	DR/CR	DR/CR	DR/CR	DR/CR	DR/CR	DR/CR
Gross credit purchases £3,390			3,390 CR	565 DR	2,825 DR			
Gross credit sales returns £1,860		1,860 CR		310 DR		1,550 DR		
Payments to credit suppliers £4,590	4,590 CR		4,590 DR					
Receipts from credit customers £5,480	5,480 DR	5,480 CR						
Discounts allowed £400		400 CR						400 DR
Discounts received £200			200 DR				200 CR	

Task 2.6

Account name	Amount £	Debit ✓	Credit ✓
Irrecoverable debts	1,560	✓	
VAT	312	✓	
Sales ledger control	1,872		✓

Chapter 3

Task 3.1

	Control account ✓	List of balances ✓	Both ✓
Invoice entered into the sales day book as £980 instead of £890			✓
Purchases day book overcast by £1,000	✓		
Discounts allowed of £20 not entered into the cash book (debit side)			✓
An invoice taken as £340 instead of £440 when being posted to the customer's account		✓	
Incorrect balancing of a memorandum ledger account		✓	
A purchases return not entered into the purchases returns day book			✓

Task 3.2

Sales ledger control

	£		£
Balance b/f	5,000	Bank (2,400 + 3,600 +1,100 + 4,800)	11,900
Sales (2,000 + 2,700 + 1,100 + 3,800)	9,600	Balance c/d	2,700
	14,600		14,600
Balance b/d	2,700		

Sales ledger

H Simms

	£		£
Balance b/f	900	Bank	2,400
Sales	2,000	Balance c/d	500
	2,900		2,900
Balance b/d	500		

P Good

	£		£
Balance b/f	1,600	Bank	3,600
Sales	2,700	Balance c/d	700
	4,300		4,300
Balance b/d	700		

K Mitchell

	£		£
Sales	1,100	Bank	1,100

C Brown

	£		£
Balance b/f	2,500	Bank	4,800
Sales	3,800	Balance c/d	1,500
	6,300		6,300
Balance b/d	1,500		

Reconciliation of sales ledger balances with control account balance

	£
H Simms	500
P Good	700
K Mitchell	
C Brown	1,500
Sales ledger control account	2,700

Task 3.3

Purchases ledger control

	£		£
Bank		Balance b/f	2,700
(1,700 + 3,200 + 3,000)	7,900	Purchases	
Balance c/d	2,100	(1,600 + 2,500 + 3,200)	7,300
	10,000		10,000
		Balance b/d	2,100

Purchases ledger

J Peters

	£		£
Bank	1,700	Balance b/f	300
Balance c/d	200	Purchases	1,600
	1,900		1,900
		Balance b/d	200

T Sands

	£		£
Bank	3,200	Balance b/f	1,700
Balance c/d	1,000	Purchases	2,500
	4,200		4,200
		Balance b/d	1,000

L Farmer

	£		£
Bank	3,000	Balance b/f	700
Balance c/d	900	Purchases	3,200
	3,900		3,900
		Balance b/d	900

Reconciliation of purchases ledger balances with control account balance

	£
J Peters	200
T Sands	1,000
L Farmer	900
Purchases ledger control account	2,100

Task 3.4

Sales ledger control

	£		£
Balance b/f	13,452	(i) Sales returns	100
		(iii) Irrecoverable debts expense	200
		Balance c/d	13,152
	13,452		13,452
Balance b/d	13,152		

	£
Sales ledger list of balances	12,614
Error: (ii) Over-statement of receipt (530 – 350)	180
Error: (iv) Balance omitted	358
Amended list of balances	13,152
Amended control account balance	13,152

Task 3.5

Purchases ledger control

	£		£
(iv) Discounts received: reversal of credit	256	Balance b/f	26,677
(iv) Discounts received: correct entry	256	(i) Purchases	1,000
Balance c/d	27,165		
	27,677		27,677
		Balance b/d	27,165

	£
Purchases ledger list of balances	27,469
Error: (ii) Discounts omitted	(64)
Error: (iii) Debit balance – remove credit balance	(120)
Error: (iii) Debit balance – enter as debit balance	(120)
Amended list of balances	27,165
Amended control account balance	27,165

Task 3.6

(a)

Sales ledger control

Date	Details	Amount £	Date	Details	Amount £
01 Nov	Balance b/f	48,125	30 Nov	Bank	28,327
30 Nov	Sales	37,008	30 Nov	Discounts allowed	240
			30 Nov	Sales returns	2,316
			30 Nov	Balance c/d	54,250
		85,133			85,133
01 Dec	Balance b/d	54,250			

(b)

	£
Sales ledger control account balance as at 1 December	54,250
Total of sales ledger accounts as at 1 December	(54,163)
Difference	87

(c) The correct answers are: A sales credit note has been entered in the sales ledger twice and A receipt from a customer has been entered in the sales ledger twice

··

Task 3.7

The correct answer is: £313

Working

VAT control

	£		£
Purchases (£4,500 × 20%)	900	Balance b/f	2,165
Van (£10,460 × 20%)	2,092	Sales (£(6,000 − 300) × 20%)	1,140
Balance c/d	313		
	3,305		3,305

··

Task 3.8

The correct answer is: £10,773.50

Workings

	£
VAT on credit sales (106,800 × 20/120)	17,800.00
VAT on sales of assets held for several years (20,100 × 20/120)	3,350.00
Less: VAT on purchases (57,810 × 20/120)	(9,635.00)
VAT on credit notes (2,820 × 20/120)	(470.00)
VAT on expenses	(271.50)
	10,773.50

Task 3.9

(a) One of either of the following reasons:

- Sales were less than purchases during the period.
- There had been an overpayment of VAT in the previous period.

(b) The correct answer is: £21,540

   Working

   £129,240 × 20/120 = £21,540

Task 3.10

(a) The correct answer is: The supplier has allowed you £150 settlement discount which you had not entered in your ledger

   All other options would lead to a higher balance in the supplier's records.

(b) The correct answer is: Both the control account and the list of balances

(c) The correct answer is: £75,355

Working

	£
Balance per listing	81,649
Less: invoice posted twice	(4,688)
Less: payments omitted	(1,606)
	75,355
Balance per control account	76,961
Less: payments omitted	(1,606)
	75,355

··

Task 3.11

(a) The correct answers are: The balance on the sales ledger control account and The total of all the sales ledger balances

(b) The correct answer is: Over how many months the outstanding balance owed by each individual credit customer has built up

··

Chapter 4

Task 4.1

(a)   The correct answer is: £297.06

Working

	£
Gross wage	440.00
PAYE income tax	(77.76)
Employees' NIC	(43.18)
Pension contribution (440.00 × 5%)	(22.00)
Net wage	297.06

(b)   The correct answers are:

£297.06 should be paid to Peter

£22.00 should be paid to the pension administrator

£170.29 (£77.76 + £43.18 + £49.35) should be paid to HM Revenue and Customs

(c)

Wages expense

	£		£
Wages control	440.00		
Wages control	49.35		

Wages control

	£		£
Bank	297.06	Wages expense	440.00
PAYE/NIC payable	77.76	Wages expense	49.35
PAYE/NIC payable	43.18		
Pension payable	22.00		
PAYE/NIC payable	49.35		

HMRC

	£		£
		Wages control	77.76
		Wages control	43.18
		Wages control	49.35

Pension payable

	£		£
		Wages control	22.00

Bank

	£		£
		Wages control	207.00

Task 4.2

Journal

Account name	Debit £	Credit £
Capital		10,000
Furniture and fittings	15,315	
Sales		127,318
Motor vehicles	20,109	
Cash at bank	15,000	
Purchases	86,120	
Purchases returns		750
Purchases ledger control		37,238
Sales ledger control	53,259	
Loan from bank		7,000
Motor expenses	1,213	
VAT		8,710
Totals	191,016	191,016

Task 4.3

Journal

Account name	Amount £	Debit ✓	Credit ✓
Irrecoverable debts expense	240	✓	
VAT (£240 × 20% = £48)	48	✓	
Sales ledger control	288		✓

Task 4.4

Journal

Account names	Amount £	Debit ✓	Credit ✓
(a)			
Discounts allowed	50	✓	
Discounts received	50		✓
(b)			
Bank deposit account	200	✓	
Bank current account	200		✓
(c)			
Irrecoverable debts expense	2,800	✓	
VAT control	560	✓	
Sales ledger control	3,360		✓

Task 4.5

Account name	Amount £	Debit ✓	Credit ✓
Irrecoverable debts expense	2,370	✓	
VAT	474	✓	
Sales ledger control	2,844		✓

Task 4.6

Account name	Amount £	Debit ✓	Credit ✓
Petty cash control	200	✓	
Cash at bank	1,000	✓	
Capital	500		✓
Van	6,000	✓	
Trade receivables	7,700	✓	
Loan from bank	9,000		✓
Sales	15,250		✓
Purchases	6,230	✓	
Trade payables	3,400		✓
Expenses	7,020	✓	
Journal to record the opening entries of new business			

Task 4.7

Account name	Amount £	Debit ✓	Credit ✓
Cash	150	✓	
Cash at bank	12,350	✓	
Capital	23,456		✓
Fixtures and fittings	2,100	✓	
Insurance	825	✓	
Loan from bank	10,000		✓
Miscellaneous expenses	218	✓	
Motor vehicle	15,650	✓	
Office expenses	613	✓	
Rent and rates	1,550	✓	
Journal to record the opening entries of new business			

Chapter 5

Task 5.1

Account name	Amount £	Debit ✓	Credit ✓
Suspense	11,081	✓	

Task 5.2

The correct answer is: Discounts allowed of £124 were only posted to the discounts allowed account.

Task 5.3

Sales ledger control

Details	£	Details	£
Balance b/f	1,683	Bank	14,228
Sales	15,899	Discounts allowed	900
		Irrecoverable debts expense	245
		Sales returns	1,467
		Balance c/d	742
	17,582		17,582

VAT

Details	£	Details	£
Purchases	1,985	Balance b/f	2,576
		Sales	2,368
Balance c/d	3,074	Purchases returns	115
	5,059		5,059

Task 5.4

(a) Journal entries

		Account	£	£
(i)	Debit	Sales ledger control	1,000	
	Credit	Suspense		1,000
(ii)	Dobit	Electricity	1,642	
	Credit	Suspense		1,642
(iii)	Debit	Discounts allowed	865	
	Credit	Suspense		865
	Debit	Discounts allowed	865	
	Credit	Suspense		865
(iv)	Debit	Sales ledger control	360	
	Credit	Bank		360
(v)	Debit	Purchases ledger control	120	
	Credit	Discounts received		120

(b)

Suspense

Details	£	Details	£
Balance b/f	4,372	(i) Sales ledger control	1,000
		(ii) Electricity	1,642
		(iii) Discounts allowed × 2	1,730
	4,372		4,372

Task 5.5

The journal

Account names		Debit £	Credit £
(a)	Sales returns	500	
	Sales		500
(b)	Office expenses	125	
	Bank		125
	Office expenses	125	
	Bank		125
(c)	Bank	29	
	Suspense	270	
	Purchases		299
	Purchases	299	
	Bank		299
(d)	Sales ledger control	388	
	Suspense		388
	Discounts allowed	388	
	Sales ledger control		388

Task 5.6

Suspense

Date	Details	Amount £	Date	Details	Amount £
01 July	Sales	945	30 June	Balance b/f	720
			01 July	Bank (rent & rates)	225
		945			945

Task 5.7

(a) The correct answer is: Credit £90

£890 should have been debited to the expense account. Instead, £980 has been debited. To bring this amount down to £890, the expense account should be credited with £90.

(b) The correct answer is: Error of omission

(c) The correct answer is: One side of a transaction has been recorded in the wrong account, and that account is of the same class as the correct account

(d) The correct answer is: The purchase of a non-current asset debited to the purchases account and credited to the supplier's account

(e) The correct answer is: Original entry

(f) The correct answer is: Debit £1,350

Workings

Suspense account

	£		£
Opening balance	1,350	Discounts allowed	7,500
Discounts received	6,150		
	7,500		7,500

(g) The correct answer is: The debit side to be £96 more than the credit side

Working

Debits will exceed credits by 2 × £48 = £96

(h)

	Yes	No
Omitting both entries for a transaction		✓
Posting the debit entry for an invoice to an incorrect expense account		✓
Omitting the debit entry for a transaction	✓	
Posting the debit entry for a transaction as a credit entry	✓	

Task 5.8

Error in the general ledger	Error disclosed by the trial balance ✓	Error NOT disclosed by the trial balance ✓
Recording a bank receipt of a cash sale on the debit side of the cash sales account	✓	
Entering an insurance expense in the administration expenses account		✓
Entering the discounts received account balance on the debit side of the trial balance	✓	
Miscasting the total column of one page of the sales returns day book	✓	
Failing to write up a dishonoured cheque in the cash book		✓
Recording discount allowed of £15 as £150 in the cash book		✓

Task 5.9

Discounts allowed

Details	Amount £	Details	Amount £
Suspense	209		

Machinery

Details	Amount £	Details	Amount £
		Motor vehicles	4,300

Motor vehicles

Details	Amount £	Details	Amount £
Machinery	4,300		

Sales ledger control

Details	Amount £	Details	Amount £
		Suspense	750

Suspense

Details	Amount £	Details	Amount £
Sales ledger control	750	Balance b/f	541
		Discounts allowed	209

Task 5.10

	Balances extracted on 30 June £	Balances at 1 July Debit £	Credit £
Machinery	82,885	82,885	
Computer equipment	41,640	41,640	
Insurance	17,520	17,520	
Bank (overdraft)	13,252		13,252
Petty cash	240	240	
Sales ledger control	241,500	247,250	
Purchases ledger control	134,686		134,686
VAT (owing to HM Revenue and Customs)	19,920		19,920
Capital	44,826		44,826
Sales	525,092		525,092
Purchases	269,400	269,400	
Purchases returns	16,272		16,272
Wages	61,680	61,680	
Maintenance expenses	3,283	3,283	
Stationery	8,049	8,049	
Rent and rates	3,466	3,466	
Heat and light	5,172	5,712	
Telephone	7,596	7,596	
Marketing expenses	5,327	5,327	
Totals		754,048	754,048

Task 5.11

(a)

(i)

Account name	Amount £	Debit ✓	Credit ✓
VAT	1,100		✓

(ii)

Account name	Amount £	Debit ✓	Credit ✓
VAT	1,000	✓	

(iii)

Account name	Amount £	Debit ✓	Credit ✓
Suspense	100	✓	

(b)

(i)

Account name	Amount £	Debit ✓	Credit ✓
Heat and light	350	✓	
Bank	350		✓

(ii)

Account name	Amount £	Debit ✓	Credit ✓
Heat and light	350	✓	
Bank	350		✓

Chapter 6

Task 6.1

	Comments
Cheque from B B Berry Ltd	Words and figures differ
Cheque from Q Q Stores	Unsigned
Cheque from Dagwell Enterprises	Payee name is incorrect – Electronics instead of Electrical
Cheque from Weller Enterprises	Dated 6 January 20X5 instead of 20X6 – this cheque is therefore out of date

Task 6.2

(a) The correct answer is: 1 December

With a BACS transfer there is no clearing period therefore the money is available immediately.

(b) The correct answer is ONE of:

There is no cheque to pay in at the bank so no need to visit the bank

Time-saving as no paying-in slip required

Greater security as no physical handling of the payment

No time delay due to the clearing system

Task 6.3

(a) A standing order would be set up to repay a bank loan in equal monthly instalments.

(b) A direct debit would be set up to make the minimum payment on a credit card by variable amounts each month.

(c) A bank overdraft would be arranged when short-term borrowing is needed.

Task 6.4

The correct answers are: Direct debit agreements and Cheque counterfoils

Task 6.5

The correct answers are: Words and figures match, and Date is not in the future

Task 6.6

The correct answer is: A building society

Task 6.7

Who is the drawee?	First National Bank
Who is the payee?	J Peterson
Who is the drawer?	F Ronald

AAT AQ2013 SAMPLE ASSESSMENT 1 CONTROL ACCOUNTS, JOURNALS AND THE BANKING SYSTEM

Time allowed: 2 hours

Control Accounts, Journals and the Banking System
AAT sample assessment 1

- You are employed by the business, Gold, as a bookkeeper.

- Gold uses a manual accounting system.

- Double entry takes place in the general ledger. Individual accounts of trade receivables and trade payables are kept in the sales and purchases ledgers as subsidiary accounts.

- The cash book and petty cash book should be treated as part of the double entry system unless the task instructions state otherwise.

- The VAT rate is 20%.

Task 1 (12 marks)

Gold has started a new business, Dee Designs, and a new set of accounts is to be opened. A partially completed journal to record the opening entries is shown below.

Complete the journal by showing whether each amount would be in the debit or credit column.

The Journal

Account name	Amount £	Debit ✓	Credit ✓
Capital	4,780		
Office expenses	1,927		
Sales	8,925		
Purchases	4,212		
Commission received	75		
Discounts received	54		
Cash at bank	1,814		
Petty cash	180		
Loan from bank	5,000		
Motor expenses	372		
Motor vehicles	9,443		
Other expenses	886		
Journal to record opening entries of new business.			

Task 2 (12 marks)

Gold pays its employees by BACS transfer every month and maintains a wages control account. A summary of last month's payroll transactions is shown below:

Payroll transactions	£
Gross wages	21,999
Income tax	5,755
Employer's NI	1,649
Employees' NI	1,476
Employees' pension contributions	750

(a) **Show the journal entries needed in the general ledger to record the wages expense.**

Account name		Amount £	Debit ✓	Credit ✓
	▼			
	▼			

Drop-down list:

Bank
Employees' NI
Employer's NI
HM Revenue and Customs
Income tax
Net wages
Pension
Wages control
Wages expense

(b) **Show the journal entries needed in the general ledger to record the net wages paid to employees.**

Account name		Amount £	Debit ✓	Credit ✓
	▼			
	▼			

Drop-down list:

Bank
Employees' NI
Employer's NI
HM Revenue and Customs
Income tax
Net wages
Pension
Wages control
Wages expense

∙∙∙

Task 3 (14 marks)

A credit customer, Jae Pih, has ceased trading, owing Gold £2,320 plus VAT.

(a) **Record the journal entries needed in the general ledger to write off the net amount and the VAT.**

Account name		Amount £	Debit ✓	Credit ✓
	▼			
	▼			
	▼			

Drop-down list:

Gold
Irrecoverable debts
Jae Pih
Purchases
Purchases ledger control
Sales
Sales ledger control
VAT

It is important to understand the types of error that are disclosed by the trial balance and those that are not.

(b) **Show which of the errors below are, or are not, disclosed by the trial balance.**

Errors	Error disclosed by the trial balance ✓	Error NOT disclosed by the trial balance ✓
Recording a bank payment for office expenses on the debit side of the office furniture account		
Recording a payment for motor expenses in the bank account, the motor expenses account and the miscellaneous expenses account. (Ignore VAT)		
Recording a payment by cheque to a credit supplier in the bank account and purchases ledger control account only		
Recording a cash payment for travel expenses in the cash account only. (Ignore VAT)		

One of the errors in (b) above can be classified as an error of principle.

(c) **Show which error is an error of principle.**

Errors	✓
Recording a bank payment for office expenses on the debit side of the office furniture account	
Recording a payment for motor expenses in the bank account, the motor expenses account and the miscellaneous expenses account. (Ignore VAT)	
Recording a payment by cheque to a credit supplier in the bank account and purchases ledger control account only	
Recording a cash payment for travel expenses in the cash account only. (Ignore VAT)	

Task 4 (12 marks)

A CHAPS payment of £12,265 for new computer equipment has been entered in the accounting records as £12,565. (Ignore VAT.)

(a) **Record the journal entries needed in the general ledger to remove the incorrect entry.**

Account name	Amount £	Debit ✓	Credit ✓
▼			
▼			

Drop-down list:

Bank
Cash
CHAPS
Computer equipment
Purchases
Suspense

(b) **Record the journal entries needed in the general ledger to record the correct entry.**

Account name	Amount £	Debit ✓	Credit ✓
▼			
▼			

Drop-down list:

Bank
Cash
CHAPS
Computer equipment
Purchases
Suspense

Task 5 (12 marks)

Gold's trial balance was extracted and did not balance. The debit column of the trial balance totalled £395,222 and the credit column totalled £395,141.

(a) **What entry would be needed in the suspense account to balance the trial balance?**

Account name	Amount £	Debit ✓	Credit ✓
Suspense			

The error in the trial balance has now been identified as arising from an incorrectly totalled VAT column in the cash book, as shown below.

Cash book

Date 20XX	Details	Bank £	Date 20XX	Details	Bank £	VAT £	Trade payables £	Cash purchases £
30 Jun	Balance b/f	14,197	30 Jun	James Jones	654	109		545
30 Jun	Baker and Co	1,445	30 Jun	BDL Ltd	6,197		6,197	
			30 Jun	Connor Smith	474	79		395
			30 Jun	Balance c/d	8,317			
	Total	15,642		Totals	15,642	269	6,197	940

(b) **Record the journal entry needed in the general ledger to remove the incorrect entry that was made from the cash book.**

Account name	Amount £	Debit ✓	Credit ✓
▼			

(c) **Record the journal entry needed in the general ledger to record the correct entry that should have been made from the cash book.**

Account name	Amount £	Debit ✓	Credit ✓
▼			

(d) **Record the journal entry needed in the general ledger to remove the suspense account balance arising from the error in the cash book.**

Account name		Amount £	Debit ✓	Credit ✓
▼				

Drop-down list:

Balance b/f
Balance c/d
Bank
Cash purchases
Suspense
Total
Trade payables
VAT

The journal is a book of prime entry.

(e) **Show ONE reason for maintaining the journal.**

	✓
To detect fraud	
To record goods bought on credit	
To record goods sold on credit	
To record non-regular transactions	

Task 6 (12 marks)

Gold's trial balance included a suspense account. All of the bookkeeping errors have now been traced and the journal entries shown below have been recorded.

Journal entries

Account name	Debit £	Credit £
Commission received	545	
Rent received		545
Suspense	985	
Legal fees		985
General repairs	3,667	
Suspense		3,667

Post the journal entries to the general ledger accounts below by writing the details and amounts in the relevant accounts.

Commission received

Details	Amount £	Details	Amount £

Rent received

Details	Amount £	Details	Amount £

Suspense

Details	Amount £	Details	Amount £
Balance b/f	2,682		

Legal fees

Details	Amount £	Details	Amount £

General repairs

Details	Amount £	Details	Amount £

Details and amounts:

Commission received

General repairs

Legal fees

Rent received

Suspense

Suspense

545		545	
985		985	
3,667		3,667	

....

Task 7 (14 marks)

On 30 June Gold extracted an initial trial balance which did not balance, and a suspense account was opened with a £962 debit balance. On 1 July journal entries were prepared to correct the errors that had been found, and clear the suspense account. The journal entries to correct the errors, and the list of balances in the initial trial balance, are shown below.

Re-draft the trial balance by placing the figures in the debit or credit column. You should take into account the journal entries which will clear the suspense account. Do not enter your figures with decimal places in this task and do not enter a zero in the empty column.

Journal entries

Account name	Debit £	Credit £
Cash	812	
Suspense		812
Bank	812	
Suspense		812

Account name	Debit £	Credit £
Suspense	331	
Sales		331
Purchases		331
Suspense	331	

Trial Balance

Account names	Balances extracted on 30 June £	Debit balances at 1 July £	Credit balances at 1 July £
Capital	20,774		
Motor vehicles	47,115		
Cash at bank	11,923		
Cash	200		
Sales ledger control	120,542		
Purchases ledger control	60,224		
VAT (owing to HM Revenue and Customs)	7,916		
Office expenses	3,216		
Sales	207,426		
Purchases	99,250		
Motor expenses	4,310		
Other expenses	8,822		
Totals			

Task 8 (14 marks)

On 28 July, Gold received the following bank statement as at 27 July.

MIDWAY BANK plc

52 The Parade, Darton, DF10 9SW

To: Gold   Account No 39103988   27 July 20XX

STATEMENT OF ACCOUNT

Date 20XX	Details	Paid out £	Paid in £	Balance £
01 July	Balance b/f			2,447 D
01 July	Standing order – City Tours	326		
01 July	Cheque 001229	781		
01 July	Direct Debit – ABC Ltd	3,425		
01 July	Counter credit		3,117	3,862 D
12 July	Cheque 001231	1,886		5,748 D
22 July	BACS transfer – Burford Ltd		22,448	
22 July	Cheque 001232	118		16,582 C
27 July	Standing order – Castle and Co	110		
27 July	Bank charges	57		16,415 C

D = Debit   C = Credit

(a) **Check the items on the bank statement against the items in the cash book.**

(b) **Enter any items into the cash book as needed.**

(c) **Total the cash book and clearly show the balance carried down at 27 July and brought down at 28 July.**

Cash book

Date 20XX	Details	Bank £	Date 20XX	Cheque Number	Details	Bank £
01 Jul	Thompson Tubes	3,117	01 Jul		Balance b/f	3,228
20 Jul	Bo Yen	316	01 Jul		City Tours	326
22 Jul	Niche Products	615	01 Jul		ABC Ltd	3,425
27 Jul	Longford Ltd	7,881	02 Jul	001231	Verve Designs	1,886
	▼		08 Jul	001232	Bal Byng	118
	▼		12 Jul	001233	Courtney and Co	4,114
	▼		12 Jul	001234	GHL Ltd	905
	▼		27 Jul		Castle and Co	110
	▼				▼	
	▼				▼	
	Total				Total	
	▼				▼	

Drop-down list:

ABC Ltd
Bal Byng
Balance b/d
Balance c/d
Bank charges
Bo Yen
Burford Ltd
Castle and Co
Cheque 001229
City Tours
Courtney and Co
GHL Ltd
Longford Ltd
Niche Products
Thompson Tubes
Verve Designs

Task 9 (14 marks)

On 28 September Gold received the following bank statement as at 27 September.

MIDWAY BANK plc

52 The Parade, Darton, DF10 9SW

| To: Gold | Account No 39103988 | 27 September 20XX |

STATEMENT OF ACCOUNT

Date 20XX	Details	Paid out £	Paid in £	Balance £
01 Sep	Balance b/f			4,104 D
01 Sep	BACS transfer – CDL Ltd		4,996	
01 Sep	Cheque 001499	1,015		123 D
04 Sep	Counter credit		2,240	2,117 C
12 Sep	Cheque 001500	486		1,631 C
22 Sep	CHAPS transfer – Conway Legal		37,400	
22 Sep	Cheque 001505	819		38,212 C
27 Sep	Cheque 001501	209		
27 Sep	Counter credit		1,081	
27 Sep	Cheque 001504	1,618		37,466 C

D = Debit   C = Credit

The cash book as at 27 September is shown below.

Cash book

Date 20XX	Details	Bank £	Date 20XX	Cheque Number	Details	Bank £
01 Sep	CDL Ltd	4,996	01 Sep		Balance b/f	5,119
04 Sep	Gifford Ltd	2,240	02 Sep	001500	Babbing Ltd	486
22 Sep	Kington Ltd	3,970	08 Sep	001501	Vym plc	209
22 Sep	Conway Legal	37,400	12 Sep	001502	Newton West	195
27 Sep	Fairway Ltd	1,081	12 Sep	001503	Welland Ltd	234
			18 Sep	001504	Hawes Ltd	1,618
			18 Sep	001505	Halthorpe Ltd	819
			18 Sep	001506	Roman plc	316

(a) **Identify the FOUR transactions that are included in the cash book but missing from the bank statement and complete the bank reconciliation statement below as at 27 September.**

Bank reconciliation statement as at 27 September 20XX	£
Balance as per bank statement	
Add:	
▼	
Total to add	
Less:	
▼	
▼	
▼	
Total to subtract	
Balance as per cash book	

Drop-down list:

Babbing Ltd
Balance b/f
Balance c/d
CDL Ltd
Cheque 001499
Conway Legal
Fairway Ltd
Gifford Ltd
Halthorpe Ltd
Hawes Ltd
Kington Ltd
Newton West
Roman plc
Vym plc
Welland Ltd

It is important to understand the security procedures for receipts from customers.

(b) **Show which TWO of the following security procedures Gold should use to ensure the security of receipts from customers.**

Security procedures	✓
Cash should be banked on a daily basis.	
Cheques should be banked on a monthly basis.	
Credit card sales vouchers should be shredded at the end of each day.	
Cash received too late to bank should be stored in a locked safe overnight.	
Cheques received too late to bank should be posted through the bank's letter box.	

Task 10 (14 marks)

The following is a summary of transactions with credit customers during the month of July.

(a) **Show whether each entry will be a debit or credit in the sales ledger control account in the general ledger.**

Sales ledger control account

Details	Amount £	Debit ✓	Credit ✓
Balance owing from credit customers at 1 July	101,912		
Money received from credit customers	80,435		
Discounts allowed	228		
Goods sold to credit customers	70,419		
Goods returned by credit customers	2,237		

The following is a summary of transactions with credit suppliers during the month of July.

(b) **Show whether each entry will be a debit or credit in the purchases ledger control account in the general ledger.**

Purchases ledger control account

Details	Amount £	Debit ✓	Credit ✓
Balance owing to credit suppliers at 1 July	61,926		
Journal debit to correct an error	550		
Goods returned to credit suppliers	1,128		
Purchases from credit suppliers	40,525		
Payments made to credit suppliers	45,763		

At the beginning of September the following balances were in the sales ledger.

Credit customers	Balances	
	Amount £	Debit/Credit
CTC Ltd	11,122	Debit
J B Estates	8,445	Debit
Koo Designs	23,119	Debit
PJB Ltd	1,225	Credit
Probyn pic	19,287	Debit
Yen Products	4,302	Debit

(c) **What should be the balance of the sales ledger control account in order for it to reconcile with the total of the balances in the sales ledger?**

Balance	✓
Credit balance b/d on 1 September of £65,050	
Debit balance b/d on 1 September of £65,050	
Credit balance b/d on 1 September of £67,500	
Debit balance b/d on 1 September of £67,500	

(d) **Show whether each of the following statements is true or false.**

Statements	True ✓	False ✓
An aged trade receivables analysis is sent to customers to inform them of the balance outstanding on their account.		
The purchases ledger control account enables a business to identify how much is owing to credit suppliers in total.		
The total of the balances in the purchases ledger should reconcile with the balance of the sales ledger control account.		

Task 11 (12 marks)

Below is a summary of transactions to be recorded in the VAT control account.

Transactions	Amount £
VAT owing from HM Revenue and Customs at 1 June	13,146
VAT total in the purchases day-book	19,220
VAT total in the sales day-book	31,197
VAT total in the purchases returns day-book	2,465
VAT total in the sales returns day-book	1,779
VAT on cash sales	1,910
VAT on petty cash payments	98
VAT refund received from HM Revenue and Customs	7,131
VAT on irrecoverable debts written off	950
VAT on the sale of office equipment	200

(a) **Show how each of the transactions will be recorded in the VAT control account in the general ledger by inputting each transaction below to the appropriate side of the VAT control account.**

VAT control

Details	Amount £	Details	Amount £

Transactions:

Balance b/f – owing from HMRC	13,146
Purchases	19,220
Sales	31,197
Purchases returns	2,465
Sales returns	1,779
Cash sales	1,910
Petty cash	98
VAT refund	7,131
Irrecoverable debts	950
Office equipment sold	200

The VAT return shows there is an amount owing from HM Revenue and Customs of £7,710.

(b) **Does the balance on the VAT control account in part (a) also show that £7,710 is owing from HM Revenue and Customs?**

	✓
Yes	
No	

(c) **Identify which ONE of the following sentences is true.**

	✓
The VAT control account is used to record the VAT amount of transactions and to help prepare the VAT return.	
The VAT control account is used to record the VAT amount of transactions but has no connection with the VAT return.	

Task 12 (12 marks)

Gold uses different forms of payment.

(a) **Show the most appropriate form of payment for each transaction below by linking each transaction on the left hand side with the appropriate right hand box.**

Transactions	Forms of payment
A quarterly payment of varying amounts for heating and lighting	Credit card
A payment of £2,115 to a credit supplier	Cash
A monthly payment of £300 for insurance	Standing order
A payment of £220,000 to buy new office premises	Cheque
A payment of £9.80 to buy tea and coffee	Direct debit
An internet payment of £595 to buy office furniture	CHAPS

It is important to understand the banking system.

(b) **Show whether the following statements are true or false.**

Statements	True ✓	False ✓
Purchases made using a debit card will result in funds being immediately transferred from Gold's bank account.		
The clearing system may result in banked funds not being available for Gold to withdraw immediately.		
Before accepting a payment by cheque from a new customer, Gold should ask the bank if there are sufficient funds in the customer's bank account.		

(c) **Complete the following sentences.**

Night safe facilities allow bank customers to (1)

▼

Organisations should have a document retention policy to (2)

▼

Banking documents that should be retained include (3)

▼

Drop-down lists:

(1) deposit valuables in a bank safety deposit box.
    deposit cash and cheques in the bank after closing.
    withdraw cash from the bank after closing.

(2) ensure documents are filed in alphabetical order.
    ensure documents are stored for the required period of time.
    ensure documents are shredded on an annual basis.

(3) statements of account from suppliers.
    statements of account from the bank.
    invoices for goods purchased on credit.

AAT AQ2013 SAMPLE ASSESSMENT 1
CONTROL ACCOUNTS, JOURNALS AND THE BANKING SYSTEM

ANSWERS

Control Accounts, Journals and the Banking System
AAT sample assessment 1

Task 1 (12 marks)

The Journal

Account name	Amount £	Debit ✓	Credit ✓
Capital	4,780		✓
Office expenses	1,927	✓	
Sales	8,925		✓
Purchases	4,212	✓	
Commission received	75		✓
Discounts received	54		✓
Cash at bank	1,814	✓	
Petty cash	180	✓	
Loan from bank	5,000		✓
Motor expenses	372	✓	
Motor vehicles	9,443	✓	
Other expenses	886	✓	

Journal to record opening entries of new business.

Task 2 (12 marks)

Gross wage + Employer NI

(a) **Working:** £21,999 + £1,649 = £23,648

Account name	Amount £	Debit ✓	Credit ✓
Wages expense	23,648	✓	
Wages control	23,648		✓

(b) **Working:** £21,999 – £5,755 – £1,476 – £750

Gross ᴵⁿᶜᵒᵐᵖ Tax EeeNi Eeepᵃⁿˢⁱᵒⁿ

Account name	Amount £	Debit ✓	Credit ✓
Wages control	14,018	✓	
Bank	14,018		✓

Task 3 (14 marks)

(a)

Account name	Amount £	Debit ✓	Credit ✓
Irrecoverable debts	2,320	✓	
VAT	464	✓	
Sales ledger control	2,784		✓

(b)

Errors	Error disclosed by the trial balance ✓	Error NOT disclosed by the trial balance ✓
Recording a bank payment for office expenses on the debit side of the office furniture account		✓
Recording a payment for motor expenses in the bank account, the motor expenses account and the miscellaneous expenses account. (Ignore VAT)	✓	
Recording a payment by cheque to a credit supplier in the bank account and purchases ledger control account only		✓
Recording a cash payment for travel expenses in the cash account only. (Ignore VAT)	✓	

(c)

Errors	✓
Recording a bank payment for office expenses on the debit side of the office furniture account	✓
Recording a payment for motor expenses in the bank account, the motor expenses account and the miscellaneous expenses account. (Ignore VAT)	
Recording a payment by cheque to a credit supplier in the bank account and purchases ledger control account only	
Recording a cash payment for travel expenses in the cash account only. (Ignore VAT)	

Task 4 (12 marks)

(a)

Account name	Amount £	Debit ✓	Credit ✓
Bank	12,565	✓	
Computer equipment	12,565		✓

(b) **Record the journal entries needed in the general ledger to record the correct entry.**

Account name	Amount £	Debit ✓	Credit ✓
Computer equipment	12,265	✓	
Bank	12,265		✓

Task 5 (12 marks)

(a)

Account name	Amount £	Debit ✓	Credit ✓
Suspense	81		✓

The error in the trial balance has now been identified as arising from an incorrectly totalled VAT column in the cash book, as shown below.

Cash book

Date 20XX	Details	Bank £	Date 20XX	Details	Bank £	VAT £	Trade payables £	Cash purchases £
30 Jun	Balance b/f	14,197	30 Jun	James Jones	654	109		545
30 Jun	Baker and Co	1,445	30 Jun	BDL Ltd	6,197		6,197	
			30 Jun	Connor Smith	474	79		395
			30 Jun	Balance c/d	8,317			
	Total	15,642		Totals	15,642	269	6,197	940

(b)

Account name	Amount £	Debit ✓	Credit ✓
VAT	269		✓

(c)

Account name	Amount £	Debit ✓	Credit ✓
VAT	188	✓	

(d)

Account name	Amount £	Debit ✓	Credit ✓
Suspense	81	✓	

(e)

	✓
To detect fraud	
To record goods bought on credit	
To record goods sold on credit	
To record non-regular transactions	✓

Task 6 (12 marks)

Commission received

Details	Amount £	Details	Amount £
Rent received	545		

Rent received

Details	Amount £	Details	Amount £
		Commission received	

Suspense

Details	Amount £	Details	Amount £
Balance b/f	2,682	General repairs	3,667
Legal fees	985		

Legal fees

Details	Amount £	Details	Amount £
		Suspense	

General repairs

Details	Amount £	Details	Amount £
Suspense	3,667		

Task 7 (14 marks)

Trial Balance

Account names	Balances extracted on 30 June £	Debit balances at 1 July £	Credit balances at 1 July £
Capital	20,774		20,774
Motor vehicles	47,115	47,115	
Cash at bank	11,923	12,735	
Cash	200	1,012	
Sales ledger control	120,542	120,542	
Purchases ledger control	60,224		60,224
VAT (owing to HM Revenue and Customs)	7,916		7,916
Office expenses	3,216	3,216	
Sales	207,426		207,757
Purchases	99,250	98,919	
Motor expenses	4,310	4,310	
Other expenses	8,822	8,822	
	Totals	296,671	296,671

Task 8 (14 marks)

Tutorial note: cheque 001229 for £781 on the bank statement was taken into account in the previous bank reconciliation, since the difference between the opening balance on the bank statement and the cash book is £3,228 – £2,447 = £781. Therefore it should not be entered again into the cash book.

Cash book

Date 20XX	Details	Bank £	Date 20XX	Cheque Number	Details	Bank £
01 Jul	Thompson Tubes	3,117	01 Jul		Balance b/f	3,228
20 Jul	Bo Yen	316	01 Jul		City Tours	326
22 Jul	Niche Products	615	01 Jul		ABC Ltd	3,425
27 Jul	Longford Ltd	7,881	02 Jul	001231	Verve Designs	1,886
22 Jul	Burford Ltd	22,448	08 Jul	001232	Bal Byng	118
			12 Jul	001233	Courtney and Co	4,114
			12 Jul	001234	GHL Ltd	905
			27 Jul		Castle and Co	110
			27 Jul		Bank charges	57
			27 Jul		Balance c/d	20,208
	Total	34,377			Total	34,377
28 Jul	Balance c/d	20,208				

Task 9 (14 marks)

(a) *Tutorial note: cheque 001499 for £1,015 on the bank statement was taken into account in the previous bank reconciliation, since the difference between the opening balance on the bank statement and the cash book is £5,119 - £4,104 = £1,015. Therefore it should not appear on the bank reconciliation.*

Bank reconciliation statement as at 27 September 20XX	£
Balance as per bank statement	37,466
Add:	
Kington Ltd	3,970
Total to add	3,970
Less:	
Newton West	195
Welland Ltd	234
Roman plc	316
Total to subtract	745
Balance as per cash book	40,691

BPP LEARNING MEDIA

(b)

Security procedures	✓
Cash should be banked on a daily basis.	✓
Cheques should be banked on a monthly basis.	
Credit card sales vouchers should be shredded at the end of each day.	
Cash received too late to bank should be stored in a locked safe overnight.	✓
Cheques received too late to bank should be posted through the bank's letter box.	

Task 10 (14 marks)

(a) **Sales ledger control account**

Details	Amount £	Debit ✓	Credit ✓
Balance owing from credit customers at 1 July	101,912	✓	
Money received from credit customers	80,435		✓
Discounts allowed	228		✓
Goods sold to credit customers	70,419	✓	
Goods returned by credit customers	2,237		✓

(b) **Purchases ledger control account**

Details	Amount £	Debit ✓	Credit ✓
Balance owing to credit suppliers at 1 July	61,926		✓
Journal debit to correct an error	550	✓	
Goods returned to credit suppliers	1,128	✓	
Purchases from credit suppliers	40,525		✓
Payments made to credit suppliers	45,763	✓	

(c)

Balance	✓
Credit balance b/d on 1 September of £65,050	
Debit balance b/d on 1 September of £65,050	✓
Credit balance b/d on 1 September of £67,500	
Debit balance b/d on 1 September of £67,500	

(d)

Statements	True ✓	False ✓
An aged trade receivables analysis is sent to customers to inform them of the balance outstanding on their account.		✓
The purchases ledger control account enables a business to identify how much is owing to credit suppliers in total.	✓	
The total of the balances in the purchases ledger should reconcile with the balance of the sales ledger control account.		✓

Task 11 (12 marks)

(a) **VAT control**

Details	Amount £	Details	Amount £
Balance b/f – owing from HMRC	13,146	Sales	31,197
Purchases	19,220	Purchases returns	2,465
Sales returns	1,779	Cash sales	1,910
Petty cash	98	VAT refund	7,131
Irrecoverable debts	950	Office equipment sold	200

35193

42903

(b) *Tutorial note: the balance is a £7,710 credit balance, that is the amount owed **to** HMRC.*

	✓
Yes	
No	✓

(c)

	✓
The VAT control account is used to record the VAT amount of transactions and to help prepare the VAT return.	✓
The VAT control account is used to record the VAT amount of transactions but has no connection with the VAT return.	

Task 12 (12 marks)

(a)

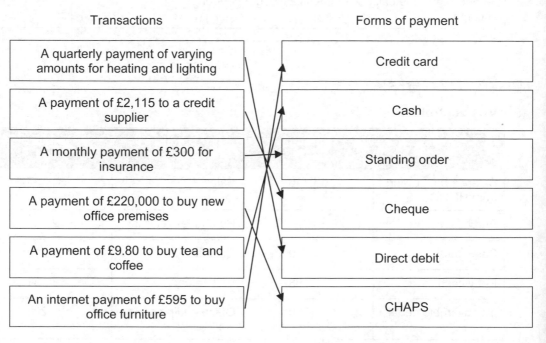

(b)

Statements	True ✓	False ✓
Purchases made using a debit card will result in funds being immediately transferred from Gold's bank account.	✓	
The clearing system may result in banked funds not being available for Gold to withdraw immediately.	✓	
Before accepting a payment by cheque from a new customer, Gold should ask the bank if there are sufficient funds in the customer's bank account.		✓

(c) Night safe facilities allow bank customers to **deposit cash and cheques in the bank after closing**.

Organisations should have a document retention policy to **ensure documents are stored for the required period of time**.

Banking documents that should be retained include **statements of account from the bank**.

AAT AQ2013 SAMPLE ASSESSMENT 2 CONTROL ACCOUNTS, JOURNALS AND THE BANKING SYSTEM

Time allowed: 2 hours

Control Accounts, Journals and the Banking System
AAT sample assessment 2

- You are employed by the business, Gold, as a bookkeeper.

- Gold uses a manual accounting system.

- Double entry takes place in the general ledger. Individual accounts of trade receivables and trade payables are kept in the sales and purchases ledgers as subsidiary accounts.

- The cash book and petty cash book should be treated as part of the double entry system unless the task instructions state otherwise.

- The VAT rate is 20%.

Task 1 (12 marks)

Gold has started a new business, FJB Products, and a new set of accounts is to be opened. A partially completed journal to record the opening entries is shown below.

Complete the journal by writing each amount in either the debit or credit column.

The Journal

Account name	Amount £	Debit £	Credit £
Capital	16,842		
Fixtures and fittings	20,476		
Bank overdraft	2,190		
Motor vehicle hire costs	1,014		
Purchases ledger control	12,444		
Cash sales	32,612		
Purchases	38,421		
Discounts received	640		
Bank deposit account	2,865		
Selling expenses	909		
Rent and rates	1,240		
Bank interest received	197		
Journal to record opening entries of new business			

Task 2 (12 marks)

Gold pays its employees by BACS transfer every month and maintains a wages control account. A summary of last month's payroll transactions is shown below:

Payroll transactions	£
Gross wages	44,769
Income tax	9,026
Employer's NI	5,371
Employees' NI	4,426
Employees' pension contributions	898
Employer's pension contributions	1,560
Trade union fees	740

(a) **Show the journal entries needed in the general ledger to record the net wages paid to employees.**

Account name		Amount £	Debit ✓	Credit ✓
	▼			
	▼			

Drop-down list:

Bank
Employees' NI
Employer's NI
HM Revenue and Customs
Income tax
Net wages
Pension
Trade union
Wages control
Wages expense

(b) **Show the journal entries needed in the general ledger to record the HM Revenue and Customs liability.**

Account name		Amount £	Debit ✓	Credit ✓
	▼			
	▼			

Drop-down list:

Bank
Employees' NI
Employer's NI
HM Revenue and Customs
Income tax
Net wages
Pension
Trade union
Wages control
Wages expense

Task 3 (14 marks)

A credit customer, Heidi Lowe, has ceased trading, owing Gold £2,046 inclusive of VAT.

(a) **Record the journal entries needed in the general ledger to write off the net amount and the VAT.**

Account name		Amount £	Debit ✓	Credit ✓
	▼			
	▼			
	▼			

Drop-down list:

Gold
Heidi Lowe
Irrecoverable debts
Purchases
Purchases ledger control
Sales
Sales ledger control
VAT

Certain types of errors are not disclosed by the trial balance.

(b) **Match each error description with the correct type of error by writing the appropriate answer in the table below. Ignore VAT.**

Error descriptions	Type of error
Recording a payment for office expenses as a debit in the bank account and a credit in the office expenses account	
Recording a bank payment for building repairs in the insurance account	

Answers:

Error of commission	Error of principle	Error of original entry
Reversal of entries	Error of omission	Compensating error

Some errors are disclosed by the trial balance.

(c) **Show whether the errors below are, or are NOT, disclosed by the trial balance by linking the left hand box with the appropriate right hand box.**

Recording cash drawings by the owner as a credit entry in both the drawings account and the cash account	Error disclosed by the trial balance
Recording rent received as a debit entry in the rent and rates account	
Recording a BACS payment to a credit supplier in the purchases ledger only	Error NOT disclosed by the trial balance

Task 4 (12 marks)

This is a note from the Accounts Manager at Gold.

Please prepare journal entries to correct an error in the accounting records.

A BACS payment for the purchase of a new computer for £5,520 has been recorded in the office expenses account (ignore VAT).

Thank you.

(a) **Record the journal entries needed in the general ledger to remove the incorrect entry.**

Account name		Amount £	Debit ✓	Credit ✓
▼				
▼				

Drop-down list:

BACS
Bank
Computer equipment
Office expenses
Purchases
Suspense

(b) **Record the journal entries needed in the general ledger to record the correct entry.**

Account name		Amount £	Debit ✓	Credit ✓
▼				
▼				

Drop-down list:

BACS
Bank
Computer equipment
Office expenses
Purchases
Suspense

Task 5 (12 marks)

Gold's trial balance was extracted and did not balance. The debit column of the trial balance totalled £426,672 and the credit column totalled £426,492.

(a) **What entry would be needed in the suspense account to balance the trial balance?**

Account name	Amount £	Debit ✓	Credit ✓
Suspense			

The error in the trial balance has now been identified as arising from an incorrectly totalled net column in the sales returns day-book, as shown below.

Sales returns day-book

Date 20XX	Details	Credit note number	Total £	VAT £	Net £
15 Jun	Conway and Co	412	378	63	315
20 Jun	AVM Ltd	413	228	38	190
29 Jun	Ziggy Designs	414	882	147	735
			1,488	248	1,420

(b) **Record the journal entry needed in the general ledger to remove the incorrect entry made from the sales returns day-book.**

Account name	Amount £	Debit ✓	Credit ✓
▼			

Drop-down list:

Net
Sales
Sales ledger control
Sales returns
Suspense
Total
VAT

(c) **Record the journal entry needed in the general ledger to record the correct entry that should have been made from the sales returns day-book.**

Account name		Amount £	Debit ✓	Credit ✓
	▼			

Drop-down list:

Net
Sales
Sales ledger control
Sales returns
Suspense
Total
VAT

(d) **Record the journal entry needed in the general ledger to remove the suspense account balance arising from the error in the sales returns day-book.**

Account name		Amount £	Debit ✓	Credit ✓
	▼			

Drop-down list:

Net
Sales
Sales ledger control
Sales returns
Suspense
Total
VAT

The journal is a book of prime entry.

(e) **Show ONE reason for maintaining the journal.**

	✓
To correct errors only	
To correct errors and record transactions that have not been recorded in any other book of prime entry	
To correct errors and record transactions from every other book of prime entry	

Task 6 (12 marks)

Gold's trial balance included a suspense account. All of the bookkeeping errors have now been traced and the journal entries shown below have been recorded.

Post the journal entries to the general ledger accounts below by writing the details and amounts in the relevant accounts.

Bank

Details	Amount £	Details	Amount £

Capital

Details	Amount £	Details	Amount £

Office equipment

Details	Amount £	Details	Amount £

Suspense

Details	Amount £	Details	Amount £
		Balance b/f	569

Sales

Details	Amount £	Details	Amount £

Details and amounts:

Bank

Capital

Office equipment

Sales

Suspense

Suspense

909

1,478

2,750

909

1,478

2,750

Journal entries

Account name	Debit £	Credit £
Bank	2,750	
Capital		2,750
Office equipment	909	
Suspense		909
Suspense	1,478	
Sales		1,478

Task 7 (14 marks)

On 30 June Gold extracted an initial trial balance which did not balance, and a suspense account was opened with an £80 credit balance. On 1 July journal entries were prepared to correct the errors that had been found, and clear the suspense account. The journal entries to correct the errors, and the list of balances in the initial trial balance, are shown below.

Re-draft the trial balance by placing the figures in the debit or credit column. You should take into account the journal entries which will clear the suspense account. Do not enter your figure with decimal places in this task and do not enter zero in the empty column.

Journal entries

Account name	Debit £	Credit £
Sales returns	960	
Suspense		960
VAT	192	
Suspense		192

Account name	Debit £	Credit £
Suspense	616	
Purchases		616
Suspense	616	
Commission received		616

Trial Balance

Account name	Balances extracted on 30 June £	Debit balances at 1 July £	Credit balances at 1 July £
Sales returns	3,071		
Capital	35,142		
Drawings by owner	1,691		
Cash at bank	3,076		
Purchases ledger control	50,216		
Sales ledger control	84,917		
VAT (owing to HM Revenue and Customs)	9,438		
Commission received	1,360		
Sales	149,111		
Purchases	119,692		
Motor vehicles	31,024		
General expenses	1,876		
Totals			

Task 8 (14 marks)

On 28 July, Gold received the following bank statement as at 27 July.

<table>
<tr><td colspan="5" align="center">MIDWAY BANK plc</td></tr>
<tr><td colspan="5" align="center">52 The Parade, Darton, DF10 9SW</td></tr>
<tr><td>To: Gold</td><td colspan="2" align="center">Account No 39103988</td><td colspan="2" align="right">27 July 20XX</td></tr>
<tr><td colspan="5" align="center">STATEMENT OF ACCOUNT</td></tr>
<tr><td>Date 20XX</td><td>Details</td><td>Paid out
£</td><td>Paid in
£</td><td>Balance
£</td></tr>
<tr><td>01 July</td><td>Balance b/f</td><td></td><td></td><td>1,994 D</td></tr>
<tr><td>01 July</td><td>Standing order – Boston Ltd</td><td>1,887</td><td></td><td></td></tr>
<tr><td>01 July</td><td>Cheque 003211</td><td>455</td><td></td><td></td></tr>
<tr><td>01 July</td><td>Direct Debit – GBL Ltd</td><td>1,973</td><td></td><td></td></tr>
<tr><td>01 July</td><td>Counter credit</td><td></td><td>8,715</td><td>2,406 C</td></tr>
<tr><td>16 July</td><td>Cheque 003223</td><td>552</td><td></td><td>1,854 C</td></tr>
<tr><td>22 July</td><td>BACS transfer – Evelyn Designs</td><td></td><td>664</td><td></td></tr>
<tr><td>22 July</td><td>Cheque 003224</td><td>1,994</td><td></td><td>524 C</td></tr>
<tr><td>27 July</td><td>Standing order – Chester Ltd</td><td>1,950</td><td></td><td></td></tr>
<tr><td>27 July</td><td>Bank charges</td><td>36</td><td></td><td>1,462 D</td></tr>
<tr><td colspan="5" align="center">D=Debit   C=Credit</td></tr>
</table>

(a) **Check the items on the bank statement against the items in the cash book.**

(b) **Enter any items into the cash book as needed.**

(c) **Total the cash book and clearly show the balance carried down at 27 July AND brought down at 28 July.**

Cash book

Date 20XX	Details	Bank £	Date 20XX	Cheque Number	Details	Bank £
01 Jul	Tristram Ltd	8,715	01 Jul		Balance b/f	2,449
20 Jul	Healy Homes	532	01 Jul		Boston Ltd	1,887
22 Jul	Grantham Ltd	140	01 Jul		GBL Ltd	1,973
27 Jul	Crowford plc	508	02 Jul	003223	Knight plc	552
	▼		08 Jul	003224	Kershaw Ltd	1,994
	▼		12 Jul	003225	JJP Ltd	346
	▼		12 Jul	003226	Malcolm Perry	884
	▼		27 Jul		Chester Ltd	1,950
	▼				▼	
	▼				▼	
	▼				▼	

Drop-down list:

Balance b/d
Balance c/d
Bank charges
Boston Ltd
Cheque 003211
Chester Ltd
Crowford plc
Evelyn Designs
GBL Ltd
Grantham Ltd
Healy Homes
JJP Ltd
Kershaw Ltd
Knight plc
Malcom Perry
Tristram Ltd

Task 9 (14 marks)

On 28 September, Gold received the following bank statement as at 27 September.

MIDWAY BANK plc

52 The Parade, Darton, DF10 9SW

To: Gold   Account No 39103988   27 September 20XX

STATEMENT OF ACCOUNT

Date 20XX	Details	Paid out £	Paid in £	Balance £
01 Sep	Balance b/f			2,379 D
02 Sep	Direct debit – Lucas Ltd	810		3,189 D
04 Sep	Cheque 017789	1,327		
04 Sep	Counter credit		7,119	2,603 C
10 Sep	Cheque 017777	606		1,997 C
21 Sep	Cheque 017791	2,772		
21 Sep	BACS transfer – Evert plc		1,966	1,191 C
25 Sep	Counter credit		1,054	2,245 C
27 Sep	Cheque 017793	882		
27 Sep	BACS transfer – Austin and Fry		1,256	2,619 C

D=Debit   C=Credit

The cash book as at 27 September is shown below.

Cash book

Date 20XX	Details	Bank £	Date 20XX	Cheque Number	Details	Bank £
04 Sep	Brian Taylor	7,119	01 Sep		Balance b/f	2,985
12 Sep	Kidson and Co	3,810	01 Sep	017789	Finch Ltd	1,327
21 Sep	Evert plc	1,966	02 Sep		Lucas Ltd	810
25 Sep	Lacey Traders	6,218	04 Sep	017790	Dee Designs	1,231
25 Sep	Scott and Smith	1,054	16 Sep	017791	Parry Partners	2,772
27 Sep	Austin and Fry	1,256	16 Sep	017792	Highbanks plc	1,122
			22 Sep	017793	Els Electrics	882

(a) **Identify the FOUR transactions that are included in the cash book but missing from the bank statement and complete the bank reconciliation statement below as at 27 September.**

Bank reconciliation statement as at 27 September 20XX	£
Balance as per bank statement	
Add:	
▼	
▼	
Total to add	
Less:	
▼	
▼	
Total to subtract	
Balance as per cash book	

Drop-down list:

Austin and Fry
Balance b/f
Balance c/d
Brian Taylor
Cheque 017777
Dee Designs
Els Electrics
Evert plc
Finch Ltd
Highbanks plc
Kidson and Co
Lacey Traders
Lucas Ltd
Parry Partners
Scott and Smith

The procedures below are an extract from Gold's cash handling policy.

(b) **Show whether each procedure will or will NOT help to ensure the security of receipts from customer.**

Procedures	Secure ✓	Not secure ✓
Cash received from customers must be held in a locked safe until banked.		
Cash received from customers should only be banked on the last day of the month.		

Task 10 (14 marks)

The following is a summary of transactions with credit customers during the month of July.

(a) **Show whether each entry will be a debit or credit in the sales ledger control account in the general ledger.**

Details of transactions	Amount £	Debit ✓	Credit ✓
Discounts allowed	255		
Irrecoverable debts written off	3,152		
Balance owing from credit customers at 1 July	99,851		
Money received from credit customers	81,334		
Journal credit to correct an error	276		
Goods returned by credit customers	422		
Goods sold to credit customers	73,996		

At the beginning of September the following balances were in the sales ledger.

Credit customer	Balances	
	Amount £	Debit/Credit
CCD Ltd	1,255	Credit
David Designs	30,821	Debit
M Davies	19,179	Debit
Norfolk Products plc	12,455	Debit
Thomas and Co	388	Debit
VWC Ltd	25,896	Debit

(b) **What should be the balance of the sales ledger control account in order for it to reconcile with the total of the balances in the sales ledger? Choose ONE answer.**

Balance	✓
Credit balance b/d on 1 September of £87,484	
Debit balance b/d on 1 September of £87,484	
Credit balance b/d on 1 September of £89,994	
Debit balance b/d on 1 September of £89,994	

The note below is from the Accounts Manager at Gold.

The total of the balances in the purchases ledger totalled £59,812 at the end of August but it has now been discovered that an invoice for £560 has been omitted from a supplier's account. The error has been corrected and should not affect the purchases ledger control account.

Please check the balance of the purchases ledger control account.

(c) **What should be the balance of the purchases ledger control account in order for it to reconcile with the corrected balance of the purchases ledger? Choose ONE answer.**

Balance	✓
Credit balance b/d on 1 September of £59,252	
Debit balance b/d on 1 September of £59,252	
Credit balance b/d on 1 September of £59,812	
Debit balance b/d on 1 September of £59,812	
Credit balance b/d on 1 September of £60,372	
Debit balance b/d on 1 September of £60,372	

(d) **Show whether the following statements are true or false.**

Statements	True ✓	False ✓
An aged trade receivables analysis is used when chasing credit customers for outstanding payments.		
An aged trade receivables analysis is sent to credit customers when outstanding payments are being requested.		
When an error is detected in the purchases ledger, the error should be corrected immediately.		
When an error is detected in the sales ledger, the error should not be corrected until the statements of account are sent to customers.		
Reconciliation of the purchases ledger control account should be carried out once every quarter.		

Task 11 (12 marks)

Below is a summary of transactions to be recorded in the VAT control account in the general ledger.

(a) **Show whether each of the transactions below will be a debit or credit entry in the VAT control account by writing each transaction in the appropriate column.**

Transactions	Amount £	Debit £	Credit £
VAT on the sale of office equipment	320		
VAT total in the purchases day-book	18,116		
VAT total in the sales day-book	33,467		
VAT on petty cash payments	544		
VAT refund received from HM Revenue and Customs	1,922		
VAT on cash sales	322		
VAT on cash purchases	198		
VAT balance b/f (owing to HM Revenue and Customs)	224		
VAT total in the purchases returns day-book	480		
VAT total in the sales returns day-book	198		
VAT on irrecoverable debts written off	9,443		

The VAT return shows there is an amount owing to HM Revenue and Customs of £22,318.

(b) **Does the balance on the VAT control account in part (a) now also show that £22,318 is owing to HM Revenue and Customs?**

	✓
Yes	
No	

Task 12 (12 marks)

Gold uses different forms of payment.

(a) **Show whether the statements below are true or false by writing the appropriate answer against each statement. You can use each answer more than once.**

Statements	True or False?
A debit card cannot be used to make purchases via the internet.	
When payment is received by cheque the amount shown in words must agree with the amount shown in figures for the cheque to be valid.	
A standing order will allow Gold to make regular payments of varying amounts.	
When payment is made by credit card the funds leave Gold's bank account immediately.	

Answers:

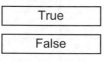

It is important to understand the banking system.

(b) **Complete the following sentences.**

An organisation's document retention policy should include a requirement for banking documents to be retained for a minimum period of [▼]

Drop-down list:

six weeks.
six months.
six years.

Banking documents that should be retained include [▼]

Drop-down list:

receipts for amounts paid into the bank.
bank reconciliation statements.
petty cash vouchers.

When Gold banks a cheque received the funds are [▼]

Drop-down list:

always available immediately.
definitely available when the cheque has cleared.
guaranteed.

Gold makes use of some of the facilities offered by the banks.

(c) **Link each facility to a description by drawing a line.**

Facilities	Descriptions
Bank loan	A facility that allows customers to gain interest on surplus funds
CHAPS	A facility that allows customers to borrow money on a long term basis
Deposit account	A facility that allows customers to borrow money on a short term flexible basis
Bank overdraft	A facility that allows customers to deposit cash and cheques after bank closing hours
Night safe	A facility that allows customers to make high value same day payments

AAT AQ2013 SAMPLE ASSESSMENT 2 CONTROL ACCOUNTS, JOURNALS AND THE BANKING SYSTEM

ANSWERS

Control Accounts, Journals and the Banking System
AAT sample assessment 2

Task 1 (12 marks)

The Journal

Account name	Amount £	Debit £	Credit £
Capital	16,842		✓
Fixtures and fittings	20,476	✓	
Bank overdraft	2,190		✓
Motor vehicle hire costs	1,014	✓	
Purchases ledger control	12,444		✓
Cash sales	32,612		✓
Purchases	38,421	✓	
Discounts received	640		✓
Bank deposit account	2,865	✓	
Selling expenses	909	✓	
Rent and rates	1,240	✓	
Bank interest received	197		✓
Journal to record opening entries of new business			

Task 2 (12 marks)

$44769 - 9026 - 4426 - 898 - 740 = 29679$

(a) net wages to employee   Gross   Income Tax   EE NI   EE pensio Trade Uni

Account name	Amount £	Debit ✓	Credit ✓
Wages control	29,679	✓	
Bank	29,679		✓

(b) HMRC ea   Income Tax   EmployerNI   Employee NI

$9026 + 5371 + 4426$

Account name	Amount £	Debit ✓	Credit ✓
Wages control	18,823	✓	
HM Revenue and Customs	18,823		✓

Task 3 (14 marks)

(a)

Account name	Amount £	Debit ✓	Credit ✓
Irrecoverable debts	1,705	✓	
VAT	341	✓	
Sales ledger control	2,046		✓

(b)

Error descriptions	Type of error
Recording a payment for office expenses as a debit in the bank account and a credit in the office expenses account	Reversal of entries
Recording a bank payment for building repairs in the insurance account	Error of commission

(c)

Recording cash drawings by the owner as a credit entry in both the drawings account and the cash account	Error disclosed by the trial balance
Recording rent received as a debit entry in the rent and rates account	
Recording a BACS payment to a credit supplier in the purchases ledger only	Error NOT disclosed by the trial balance

Tutorial note: If the BACS payment was omitted from the cash book then it will not be recorded in either the Bank account or the PLCA, so the error would not be disclosed in the trial balance. AAT makes this assumption in its answer. The suggestion therefore is that either the entry has been made in the purchases ledger from a cash book that is not itself part of the double entry system, or the payment has just not been recorded at all in a book or prime entry before being entered as a debit in the purchases ledger.

Task 4 (12 marks)

(a)

Account name	Amount £	Debit ✓	Credit ✓
Bank	5,520	✓	
Office expenses	5,520		✓

(b)

Account name	Amount £	Debit ✓	Credit ✓
Bank	5,520		✓
Computer equipment	5,520	✓	

Task 5 (12 marks)

(a)

Account name	Amount £	Debit ✓	Credit ✓
Suspense	180		✓

(b)

Account name	Amount £	Debit ✓	Credit ✓
Sales returns	1,420		✓

(c)

Account name	Amount £	Debit ✓	Credit ✓
Sales returns	1,240	✓	

(d)

Account name	Amount £	Debit ✓	Credit ✓
Suspense	180	✓	

(e)

	✓
To correct errors only	
To correct errors and record transactions that have not been recorded in any other book of prime entry	✓
To correct errors and record transactions from every other book of prime entry	

Task 6 (12 marks)

Bank

Details	Amount £	Details	Amount £
Capital	2,750		

Capital

Details	Amount £	Details	Amount £
		Bank	2,750

Office equipment

Details	Amount £	Details	Amount £
Suspense	909		

Suspense

Details	Amount £	Details	Amount £
Sales	1,478	Balance b/f	569
		Office equipment	909

Sales

Details	Amount £	Details	Amount £
		Suspense	1,478

Task 7 (14 marks)

Trial Balance

Account names	Balances extracted on 30 June £	Debit balances at 1 July £	Credit balances at 1 July £
Sales returns	3,071	4,031	
Capital	35,142		35,142
Drawings by owner	1,691	1,691	
Cash at bank	3,076	3,076	
Purchases ledger control	50,216		50,216
Sales ledger control	84,917	84,917	
VAT (owing to HM Revenue and Customs)	9,438		9,246
Commission received	1,360		1,976
Sales	149,111		149,111
Purchases	119,692	119,076	
Motor vehicles	31,024	31,024	
General expenses	1,876	1,876	
Totals		**245,691**	**245,691**

Task 8 (14 marks)

Cash book

Date 20XX	Details	Bank £	Date 20XX	Cheque Number	Details	Bank £
01 Jul	Tristram Ltd	8,715	01 Jul		Balance b/f	2,449
20 Jul	Healy Homes	532	01 Jul		Boston Ltd	1,887
22 Jul	Grantham Ltd	140	01 Jul		GBL Ltd	1,973
27 Jul	Crowford plc	508	02 Jul	003223	Knight plc	552
22 Jul	Evelyn Designs	664	08 Jul	003224	Kershaw Ltd	1,994
27 Jul	Balance c/d	1,512	12 Jul	003225	JJP Ltd	346
			12 Jul	003226	Malcolm Perry	884
			27 Jul		Chester Ltd	1,950
			27 Jul		Bank charges	36
		12,071				12,071
			28 Jul		Balance b/d	1,512

Task 9 (14 marks)

(a)

Bank reconciliation statement as at 27 September 20XX	£
Balance as per bank statement	2,619
Add:	
Kidson and Co	3,810
Lacey Traders	6,218
Total to add	10,028
Less:	
Dee Designs	1,231
Highbanks plc	1,122
Total to subtract	2,353
Balance as per cash book	10,294

(b)

Procedures	Secure ✓	Not secure ✓
Cash received from customers must be held in a locked safe until banked.	✓	
Cash received from customers should only be banked on the last day of the month.		✓

Task 10 (14 marks)

(a)

Details of transactions	Amount £	Debit ✓	Credit ✓
Discounts allowed	255		✓
Irrecoverable debts written off	3,152		✓
Balance owing from credit customers at 1 July	99,851	✓	
Money received from credit customers	81,334		✓
Journal credit to correct error	276		✓
Goods returned by credit customers	422		✓
Goods sold to credit customers	73,996	✓	

(b)

Working: £(30,821 + 19,179 + 12,455 + 388 + 25,896 − 1,255) = £87,484

Balance	✓
Credit balance b/d on 1 September of £87,484	
Debit balance b/d on 1 September of £87,484	✓
Credit balance b/d on 1 September of £89,994	
Debit balance b/d on 1 September of £89,994	

(c)

Working: £(59,812 + 560) = £60,372

Balance	✓
Credit balance b/d on 1 September of £59,252	
Debit balance b/d on 1 September of £59,252	
Credit balance b/d on 1 September of £59,812	
Debit balance b/d on 1 September of £59,812	
Credit balance b/d on 1 September of £60,372	✓
Debit balance b/d on 1 September of £60,372	

(d)

Statements	True ✓	False ✓
An aged trade receivables analysis is used when chasing credit customers for outstanding payments.	✓	
An aged trade receivables analysis is sent to credit customers when outstanding payments are being requested.		✓
When an error is detected in the purchases ledger, the error should be corrected immediately.	✓	
When an error is detected in the sales ledger, the error should not be corrected until the statements of account are sent to customers.		✓
Reconciliation of the purchases ledger control account should be carried out once every quarter.		✓

Task 11 (12 marks)

(a)

Transactions	Amount £	Debit £	Credit £
VAT on the sale of office equipment	320		✓
VAT total in the purchases day-book	18,116	✓	
VAT total in the sales day-book	33,467		✓
VAT on petty cash payments	544	✓	
VAT refund received from HM Revenue and Customs	1,922		✓
VAT on cash sales	322		✓
VAT on cash purchases	198	✓	
VAT balance b/f (owing to HM Revenue and Customs)	224		✓
VAT total in the purchases returns day-book	480		✓
VAT total in the sales returns day-book	198	✓	
VAT on irrecoverable debts written off	9,443	✓	

(b) **Working:** £(320 + 33,467 + 1,922 + 322 + 224 + 480 − 18,116 − 544 − 198 − 198 − 9,443) = £8,236

	✓
Yes	
No	✓

Task 12 (12 marks)

(a)

Statements	True or False?
A debit card cannot be used to make purchases via the internet.	False
When payment is received by cheque the amount shown in words must agree with the amount shown in figures for the cheque to be valid.	True
A standing order will allow Gold to make regular payments of varying amounts.	False
When payment is made by credit card the funds leave Gold's bank account immediately.	False

(b)

An organisation's document retention policy should include a requirement for banking documents to be retained for a minimum period of six years.

Banking documents that should be retained include

receipts for amounts paid into the bank.

When Gold banks a cheque received the funds are

definitely available when the cheque has cleared.

(c)

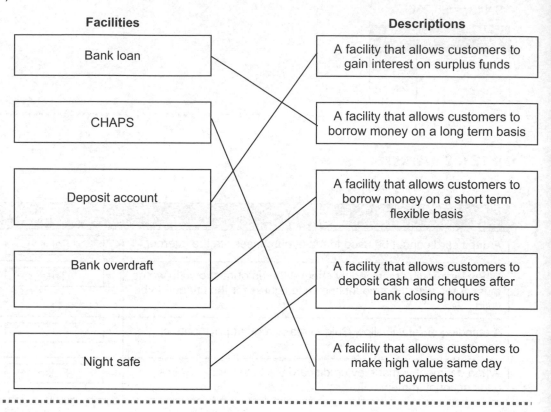

Facilities	Descriptions
Bank loan	A facility that allows customers to gain interest on surplus funds
CHAPS	A facility that allows customers to borrow money on a long term basis
Deposit account	A facility that allows customers to borrow money on a short term flexible basis
Bank overdraft	A facility that allows customers to deposit cash and cheques after bank closing hours
Night safe	A facility that allows customers to make high value same day payments

BPP PRACTICE ASSESSMENT 1 CONTROL ACCOUNTS, JOURNALS AND THE BANKING SYSTEM

Time allowed: 2 hours

Control Accounts, Journals and the Banking System
BPP practice assessment 1

- You are employed by the business, Russell Hardware, as a bookkeeper.

- Russell Hardware uses a manual accounting system.

- Double entry takes place in the general ledger. Individual accounts of trade receivables and trade payables are kept In the sales and purchases ledgers as subsidiary accounts.

- The cash book and petty cash book should be treated as part of the double entry system unless the task instructions state otherwise.

- The VAT rate is 20%.

Task 1

Russell Hardware has started a new business, Russell Giftware, and a new set of accounts is to be opened. A partially completed journal to record the opening balances is shown below.

Record the journal entries needed in the accounts in the general ledger of Russell Giftware to deal with the opening balances.

Account name	Amount £	Debit ✓	Credit ✓
Capital	10,000		
Cash at bank	2,500		
Computer	750		
Furniture and fittings	950		
Heat and light	100		
Loan from bank	5,000		
Office expenses	320		
Petty cash	200		
Purchases	9,680		
Rent and rates	500		
Journal to record the opening entries of new business			

Task 2

Russell Hardware pays its employees by BACS transfer every month and maintains a wages control account. A summary of last month's payroll transactions is shown below:

Item	£
Gross wages	7,450
Employees' NI	682
Income tax	1,204
Employees' pension contributions	90
Employer's NI	809

Record the journal entries needed in the general ledger to:

(a) **Record the HM Revenue and Customs liability**

Account name		Amount £	Debit ✓	Credit ✓
	▼			
	▼			

(b) **Record the net wages paid to the employees**

Account name		Amount £	Debit ✓	Credit ✓
	▼			
	▼			

Picklist:

Bank
Employees' NI
Employer's NI
HM Revenue and Customs
Income tax
Net wages
Pension
Wages control
Wages expense

Task 3

A credit customer, Jensen Ltd, has ceased trading, owing Russell Hardware £1,120 plus VAT.

(a) **Record the journal entries needed in the general ledger to write off the net amount and the VAT.**

Account name	Amount £	Debit ✓	Credit ✓
▼			
▼			
▼			

Picklist:

Irrecoverable debts
Jensen Ltd
Russell Hardware
Purchases
Purchases ledger control
Sales
Sales ledger control
VAT

It is important to understand the types of error that are disclosed by the trial balance and those that are not.

(b) **Show which of the errors below are, or are not, disclosed by the trial balance.**

Error in the general ledger	Error disclosed by the trial balance ✓	Error NOT disclosed by the trial balance ✓
Writing in the balance on the office stationery account incorrectly		
Recording a purchase from a credit supplier for £5,000 (no VAT) as £500 in both the purchases and the purchases ledger control accounts		
Recording a receipt from a credit customer in the cash sales account		
Recording a credit note from a supplier on the debit side of the purchases ledger control account and the debit side of the purchases returns account		

One of the errors in (b) above can be classified as error of original entry.

(c) **Show which error is an error of original entry.**

Error in the general ledger	✓
Writing in the balance on the office stationery account incorrectly	
Recording a purchase from a credit supplier for £5,000 (no VAT) as £500 in both the purchases and the purchases ledger control accounts	
Recording a receipt from a credit customer in the cash sales account	
Recording a credit note from a supplier on the debit side of the purchases ledger control account and the debit side of the purchases returns account	

Task 4

An entry to record a cheque of £352 for premises repairs (VAT not applicable) has been reversed.

(a) **Record the journal entries needed in the general ledger to remove the incorrect entry.**

Account name		Amount £	Debit ✓	Credit ✓
	▼			
	▼			

(b) **Record the journal entries needed in the general ledger to record the correct entry.**

Account name		Amount £	Debit ✓	Credit ✓
	▼			
	▼			

Picklist:

Bank
Cash
Cheque
Premises repairs
Purchases
Suspense

164

Task 5

Russell Hardware's trial balance for May was extracted and did not balance. The debit column of the trial balance totalled £297,564 and the credit column totalled £295,128.

(a) **What entry would be made in the suspense account to balance the trial balance?**

Account name	Amount £	Debit ✓	Credit ✓
Suspense			

Russell Hardware's initial trial balance for June includes a suspense account with a debit balance of £396.

The error has been traced to the total of the purchases day book shown below.

Purchases day book

Date 20XX	Details	Invoice number	Total £	VAT £	Net £
30 Jun	Fixit Ltd	8932	6,000	1,000	5,000
30 Jun	Frame Products Ltd	1092	912	152	760
30 Jun	SDF plc	663	1,536	256	1,280
	Totals		8,844	1,408	7,040

(b) **Record the journal entry needed in the general ledger to remove the incorrect entry that was made from the purchases day book.**

Account name	Amount £	Debit ✓	Credit ✓
▼			

(c) **Record the journal entry needed in the general ledger to record the correct entry that should have been made from the purchases day book.**

Account name	Amount £	Debit ✓	Credit ✓
▼			

(d) **Record the journal entry needed in the general ledger to remove the suspense account balance arising from the error in the purchases day book.**

Account name	Amount £	Debit ✓	Credit ✓
▼			

BPP
LEARNING MEDIA

Picklist:

Balance b/f
Balance c/d
Purchases
Purchases day book
Purchases ledger control
Suspense
Total
VAT

(e) **Identify whether the following statement is true or false.**

	True ✓	False ✓
A journal entry to correct an error in posting from a day book will always involve an entry in the suspense account.		

Task 6

Russell Hardware's trial balance included a suspense account. All the bookkeeping errors have now been traced and the journal entries shown below have been recorded.

Journal entries

Account name	Debit £	Credit £
Irrecoverable debts	73	
Suspense		73
Heat and light	150	
Office expenses		150
Suspense	201	
Marketing expenses		201

Post the journal entries to the general ledger accounts.

Irrecoverable debts

Details	Amount £	Details	Amount £
▼		▼	

Heat and light

Details	Amount £	Details	Amount £
▼		▼	

Marketing expenses

Details	Amount £	Details	Amount £
▼		▼	

Office expenses

Details	Amount £	Details	Amount £
▼		▼	

Suspense

Details	Amount £	Details	Amount £
▼		Balance b/f	128
▼		▼	

Picklist for line items:

Balance b/d
Irrecoverable debts
Heat and light
Marketing expenses
Office expenses
Suspense

Task 7

On 30 June Russell Hardware extracted an initial trial balance which did not balance, and a suspense account with a credit balance of £420 was opened. On 1 July journal entries were prepared to correct the errors that had been found, and clear the suspense account. The journal entries to correct the errors, and the list of balances in the initial trial balance, are shown below.

Journal entries

Account name	Debit £	Credit £
Purchases ledger control		507
Suspense	507	
Purchases ledger control		507
Suspense	507	

Account name	Debit £	Credit £
Heat and light		1,056
Suspense	1,056	
Heat and light	1,650	
Suspense		1,650

Taking into account the journal entries, which will clear the suspense account, re-draft the trial balance by writing the figures in the debit or credit column. Do not enter your figures with decimal places in this task and do not enter a zero in the empty column.

	Balances extracted on 30 June £	Balances at 1 July	
		Debit £	Credit £
Motor vehicles	13,920		
Furniture and fittings	9,208		
Inventory	10,129		
Cash at bank	673		
Petty cash	250		
Sales ledger control	7,832		
Purchases ledger control	4,292		
VAT (owing to HM Revenue and Customs)	1,029		
Capital	10,000		
Sales	89,125		
Purchases	35,268		
Purchases returns	1,092		

	Balances extracted on 30 June £	Balances at 1 July	
		Debit £	Credit £
Wages	18,279		
Marketing expenses	1,290		
Office expenses	3,287		
Rent and rates	2,819		
Heat and light	1,056		
Irrecoverable debts	127		
Motor expenses	1,820		
Totals			

Task 8

On 24 June Russell Hardware received the following bank statement as at 23 June.

Far Bank PLC

100 High Street, Manson, MN3 3KJ

To: Russell Hardware   Account No 76938472   23 June 20XX

Statement of Account

Date 20XX	Detail	Paid out £	Paid in £	Balance £	
04 June	Balance b/f			3,745	C
04 June	Cheque 109829	4,534		789	D
04 June	Cheque 109830	934		1,723	D
05 June	Cheque 109831	629		2,352	D
06 June	Cheque 109833	1,000		3,352	D
12 June	Bank Giro Credit Vista		2,019	1,333	D
13 June	Cheque 109834	643		1,976	D
13 June	Direct Debit Manson DC	200		2,176	D
20 June	Direct Debit Jaspar	760		2,936	D
23 June	Bank charges	34		2,970	D
23 June	Overdraft fee	50		3,020	D
23 June	Counter credit		3,209	189	C

D = Debit   C = Credit

(a) **Check the items on the bank statement against the items in the cash book.**

(b) **Enter any items in the cash book as needed.**

(c) **Total the cash book and clearly show the balance carried down at 23 June and brought down at 24 June.**

Cash book

Date 20XX	Details	Bank £	Date 20XX	Cheque number	Details	Bank £
01 June	Balance b/f	3,745	01 June	109829	Walker Ltd	4,534
20 June	Striss Ltd	3,209	01 June	109830	Jobber Dee plc	934
21 June	Ladbrake Ltd	1,729	01 June	109831	Street Fare Ltd	629
22 June	Crubbs & Co	3,222	01 June	109832	Urban Mass Ltd	562
	▼		02 June	109833	Ostley Ltd	1,000
	▼		02 June	109834	Quister plc	643
	▼		13 June	109835	Green Grass Ltd	98
	▼		20 June		Jaspar Properties	760
	▼				▼	
	▼				▼	
	▼				▼	
	▼				▼	
	Total				Total	
	▼				▼	

Picklist:

Balance b/d	Ostley Ltd
Balance c/d	Overdraft fee
Bank charges	Quister plc
Crubbs & Co	Street Fare Ltd
Green Grass Ltd	Striss Ltd
Jaspar Properties	Urban Mass Ltd
Jobber Dee plc	Vista plc
Ladbrake Ltd	Walker Ltd
Manson DC	

Task 9

(a) On 24 August Russell Hardware received the following bank statement as at 23 August.

Far Bank PLC

100 High Street, Manson, MN3 3KJ

To: Russell Hardware   Account No 76938472   23 August 20XX

Statement of Account

Date	Detail	Paid out	Paid in	Balance	
20XX		£	£	£	
01 Aug	Balance b/f			1,084	C
02 Aug	Cheque 110212	3,240		2,156	D
04 Aug	Cheque 110213	588		2,744	D
06 Aug	Cheque 110214	61		2,805	D
06 Aug	BGC Striss Ltd		4,547	1,742	C
17 Aug	Cheque 110217	347		1,395	C
19 Aug	BGC Crubbs & Co		1,745		
19 Aug	Cheque 110216	689		2,451	C
20 Aug	Counter credit		3,996	6,447	C
22 Aug	Cheque 110218	2,547		3,900	C
23 Aug	Cheque 110219	1,777		2,123	C

D = Debit   C = Credit   BGC = Bank Giro Credit

Cash book

Date 20XX	Details	Bank £	Date 20XX	Cheque number	Details	Bank £
6 Aug	Striss Ltd	4,547	1 Aug		Balance b/f	2,156
15 Aug	Bundle Ltd	3,996	1 Aug	110213	Ostley Ltd	588
20 Aug	Crubbs & Co	1,745	4 Aug	110214	Urban Mass Ltd	61
21 Aug	Ladbrake Ltd	10,834	7 Aug	110215	Street Fare Ltd	3,547
22 Aug	Ormskirk plc	314	9 Aug	110216	Jobber Dee plc	689
			14 Aug	110217	Walker Ltd	347
			17 Aug	110218	Jaspar Properties	2,547
			19 Aug	110219	Green Grass Ltd	1,777
			20 Aug	110220	Quister plc	32

Identify the FOUR transactions that are included in the cash book but missing from the bank statement and complete the bank reconciliation statement below as at 27 September.

Bank reconciliation statement as at 23 August 20XX		£
Balance per bank statement		
Add:		
	▼	
	▼	
Total to add		
Less:		
	▼	
	▼	
Total to subtract		
Balance as per cash book		

Picklist:

Balance b/d
Balance c/d
Bank charges
Bundle Ltd
Crubbs & Co
Green Grass Ltd
Jaspar Properties
Jobber Dee plc
Ladbrake Ltd
Manson DC
Ormskirk plc
Ostley Ltd
Overdraft fee
Quister plc
Street Fare Ltd
Striss Ltd
Urban Mass Ltd
Vista plc
Walker Ltd

(b) **Show whether each of the statements below is True or False.**

	True ✓	False ✓
When Russell Hardware makes a payment to a supplier by cheque, the amount leaves the business's bank current account immediately the supplier receives the cheque.		
When Russell Hardware makes a payment to a supplier by credit card, the amount paid does not affect the bank current account.		
When Russell Hardware makes a payment to a supplier by debit card, a charge for this service is always made by the supplier's bank to Russell Hardware.		

Task 10

This is a summary of transactions with customers during the month of June.

(a) **Show whether each entry will be a debit or credit in the sales ledger control account in the general ledger.**

Sales ledger control account

Details	Amount £	Debit ✓	Credit ✓
Balance of trade receivables at 1 June	10,298		
Goods sold on credit	13,289		
Payments received from credit customers	15,296		
Discounts allowed	425		
Goods returned by credit customers	1,046		

(b) **What will be the balance brought down on 1 July on the above account?**

	✓
Debit £6,820	
Credit £6,820	
Debit £9,762	
Credit £9,762	
Debit £10,834	
Credit £10,834	

The following debit balances were in the sales ledger on 1 July.

	£
Kendrick plc	928
Askwith Ltd	102
Raston Permanent Ltd	1,652
Biomass plc	73
Nistral plc	2,009
Larkmead & Co	1,999

(c) **Complete the following table to reconcile the balances shown above with the sales ledger control account balance you have calculated in part (b).**

	£
Sales ledger control account balance as at 30 June	
Total of sales ledger accounts as at 30 June	
Difference	

(d) **What may have caused the difference you calculated in part (c)?**

	✓
Goods returned may have been omitted from the sales ledger	
Discounts allowed may have been omitted from the sales ledger	
Goods returned may have been entered in the sales ledger twice	
Sales invoices may have been entered in the sales ledger twice	

It is important to reconcile the sales ledger control account on a regular basis.

(e) **Which ONE of the following statements is True?**

	✓
Reconciliation of the sales ledger control account assures managers that the amount showing as outstanding from customers is correct.	
Reconciliation of the sales ledger control account assures managers that the amount showing as outstanding to suppliers is correct.	
Reconciliation of the sales ledger control account will show if a purchases invoice has been omitted from the purchases ledger.	
Reconciliation of the sales ledger control account will show if a sales invoice has been omitted from the purchases ledger.	

Task 11

The following is an extract from Russell Hardware's books of prime entry.

Totals for quarter		
Sales day book		**Purchases day book**
Net: £18,725		Net: £11,025
VAT: £3,745		VAT: £2,205
Gross: £22,470		Gross: £13,230
Sales returns day book		**Purchases returns day book**
Net: £1,925		Net: £700
VAT: £385		VAT: £140
Gross: £2,310		Gross: £840
Cash book		
Net cash sales:	£350	
VAT:	£70	
Gross cash sales:	£420	

(a) **What will be the entries in the VAT control account to record the VAT transactions in the quarter?**

VAT control

Details	Amount £	Details	Amount £
▼		▼	
▼		▼	
▼		▼	

Picklist:

Cash book
Cash sales
Purchases
Purchases day book
Purchases returns
Purchases returns day book
Sales
Sales day book
Sales returns
Sales returns day book
VAT

The VAT return has been completed and shows an amount owing to HM Revenue and Customs of £1,365.

(b) **Is the VAT return correct?**

	✓
Yes	
No	

Task 12

(a) **From the list below identify TWO methods of making a non-automated payment.**

Service	Method of making non-automated payment? ✓
Cheque	
BACS	
Cash	
Direct debit	
CHAPS	

(b) **Show whether each of the following statements about banking services is True or False.**

	True ✓	False ✓
A customer with a current account at a bank will usually be able to operate it with a debit card.		
An overdraft is an arrangement whereby the customer can withdraw more money from the account than they have in it up to a certain limit.		
A dishonoured cheque is sent back to the payee's bank so that the payee can pursue payment in some other way.		
A cheque drawn on Bank A and paid in at Bank B will normally take four days to be paid.		
A customer with a credit balance on its cash book must have a bank statement that shows a credit balance.		
An aged trade receivables analysis will assist a business when reconciling its bank statement to its cash book.		

BPP PRACTICE ASSESSMENT 1
CONTROL ACCOUNTS, JOURNALS AND THE BANKING SYSTEM

ANSWERS

Control Accounts, Journals and the Banking System
BPP practice assessment 1

Task 1

Account name	Amount £	Debit ✓	Credit ✓
Capital	10,000		✓
Cash at bank	2,500	✓	
Computer	750	✓	
Furniture and fittings	950	✓	
Heat and light	100	✓	
Loan from bank	5,000		✓
Office expenses	320	✓	
Petty cash	200	✓	
Purchases	9,680	✓	
Rent and rates	500	✓	
Journal to record the opening entries of new business			

Task 2

(a)

Account name	Amount £	Debit ✓	Credit ✓
Wages control	2,695	✓	
HM Revenue and Customs	2,695		✓

(b)

Account name	Amount £	Debit ✓	Credit ✓
Wages control	5,474	✓	
Bank	5,474		✓

Task 3

(a)

Account name	Amount £	Debit	Credit
Irrecoverable debts	1,120	✓	
VAT	224	✓	
Sales ledger control	1,344		✓

(b)

Error in the general ledger	Error disclosed by the trial balance ✓	Error NOT disclosed by the trial balance ✓
Writing in the balance on the office stationery account incorrectly	✓	
Recording a purchase from a credit supplier for £5,000 (no VAT) as £500 in both the purchases and the purchases ledger control accounts		✓
Recording a receipt from a credit customer in the cash sales account		✓
Recording a credit note from a supplier on the debit side of the purchases ledger control account and the debit side of the purchases returns account	✓	

(c)

Error in the general ledger	✓
Writing in the balance on the office stationery account incorrectly	
Recording a purchase from a credit supplier for £5,000 (no VAT) as £500 in both the purchases and the purchases ledger control accounts	✓
Recording a receipt from a credit customer in the cash sales account	
Recording a credit note from a supplier on the debit side of the purchases ledger control account and the debit side of the purchases returns account	

Task 4

(a)

Account name	Amount £	Debit ✓	Credit ✓
Premises repairs	352	✓	
Bank	352		✓

(b)

Account name	Amount £	Debit ✓	Credit ✓
Premises repairs	352	✓	
Bank	352		✓

Task 5

(a)

Account name	Amount £	Debit ✓	Credit ✓
Suspense	2,436		✓

(b)

Account name	Amount £	Debit ✓	Credit ✓
Purchases ledger control	8,844	✓	

(c)

Account name	Amount £	Debit ✓	Credit ✓
Purchases ledger control	8,448		✓

(d)

Account name	Amount £	Debit ✓	Credit ✓
Suspense	396		✓

(e)

	True ✓	False ✓
A journal entry to correct an error in posting from a day book will always involve an entry in the suspense account.		✓

Task 6

Irrecoverable debts

Details	Amount £	Details	Amount £
Suspense	73		

Heat and light

Details	Amount £	Details	Amount £
Office expenses	150		

Marketing expenses

Details	Amount £	Details	Amount £
		Suspense	201

Office expenses

Details	Amount £	Details	Amount £
		Heat and light	150

Suspense

Details	Amount £	Details	Amount £
Marketing expenses	201	Balance b/f	128
		Irrecoverable debts	73

Task 7

	Balances extracted on 30 June £	Balances at 1 July	
		Debit £	Credit £
Motor vehicles	13,920	13,920	
Furniture and fittings	9,208	9,208	
Inventory	10,129	10,129	
Cash at bank	673	673	
Petty cash	250	250	
Sales ledger control	7,832	7,832	
Purchases ledger control	4,292		5,306
VAT (owing to HM Revenue and Customs)	1,029		1,029
Capital	10,000		10,000
Sales	89,125		89,125
Purchases	35,268	35,268	
Purchases returns	1,092		1,092
Wages	18,279	18,279	
Marketing expenses	1,290	1,290	
Office expenses	3,287	3,287	
Rent and rates	2,819	2,819	
Heat and light	1,056	1,650	
Irrecoverable debts	127	127	
Motor expenses	1,820	1,820	
Totals		106,552	106,552

Task 8

(a) – (c)

Cash book

Date 20XX	Details	Bank £	Date 20XX	Cheque number	Details	Bank £
01 June	Balance b/f	3,745	01 June	109829	Walker Ltd	4,534
20 June	Striss Ltd	3,209	01 June	109830	Jobber Dee plc	934
21 June	Ladbrake Ltd	1,729	01 June	109831	Street Fare Ltd	629
22 June	Crubbs & Co	3,222	01 June	109832	Urban Mass Ltd	562
12 June	Vista plc	2,019	02 June	109833	Ostley Ltd	1,000
			02 June	109834	Quister plc	643
			13 June	109835	Green Grass Ltd	98
			20 June		Jaspar Properties	760
			13 June		Manson DC	200
			23 June		Bank charges	34
			23 June		Overdraft fee	50
			23 June		Balance c/d	4,480
	Total	13,924			Total	13,924
24 June	Balance b/d	4,480				

Task 9

(a)

Bank reconciliation statement as at 23 August 20XX	£
Balance per bank statement	2,123
Add:	
Ladbrake Ltd	10,834
Ormskirk plc	314
Total to add	11,148
Less:	
Street Fare Ltd	3,547
Quister plc	32
Total to subtract	3,579
Balance as per cash book	9,692

(b)

	True ✓	False ✓
When Russell Hardware makes a payment to a supplier by cheque, the amount leaves the business's bank current account immediately the supplier receives the cheque.		✓
When Russell Hardware makes a payment to a supplier by credit card, the amount paid does not affect the bank current account.	✓	
When Russell Hardware makes a payment to a supplier by debit card, a charge for this service is always made by the supplier's bank to Russell Hardware.		✓

Task 10

(a) Sales ledger control account

Details	Amount £	Debit ✓	Credit ✓
Balance of receivables at 1 June	10,298	✓	
Goods sold on credit	13,289	✓	
Payments received from credit customers	15,296		✓
Discounts allowed	425		✓
Goods returned by credit customers	1,046		✓

(b) The correct answer is: Debit £6,820

(c)

	£
Sales ledger control account balance as at 30 June	6,820
Total of sales ledger accounts as at 30 June	6,763
Difference	57

(d) The correct answer is: Goods returned may have been entered in the sales ledger twice

(e) The correct answer is: Reconciliation of the sales ledger control account assures managers that the amount showing as outstanding from customers is correct

Task 11

(a)

VAT control

Details	Amount £	Details	Amount £
Sales returns	385	Sales	3,745
Purchases	2,205	Purchases returns	140
		Cash sales	70

(b) The correct answer is: Yes

Task 12

(a) The correct answers are: Cheque and Cash

(b)

	True ✓	False ✓
A customer with a current account at a bank will usually be able to operate it with a debit card	✓	
An overdraft is an arrangement whereby the customer can withdraw more money from the account than he has in it up to a certain limit	✓	
A dishonoured cheque is sent back to the payee's bank so that the payee can pursue payment in some other way	✓	
A cheque drawn on Bank A and paid in at Bank B will normally take four days to be paid		✓
A customer with a credit balance on its cash book must have a bank statement that shows a credit balance		✓
An aged trade receivables analysis will assist a business when reconciling its bank statement to its cash book		✓

BPP PRACTICE ASSESSMENT 2
CONTROL ACCOUNTS, JOURNALS AND THE BANKING SYSTEM

Time allowed: 2 hours

Control Accounts, Journals and the Banking System
BPP practice assessment 2

- You are employed by the business, Finn Clothing, as a bookkeeper.

- Finn Clothing uses a manual accounting system.

- Double entry takes place in the general ledger. Individual accounts of trade receivables and trade payables are kept in the sales and purchases ledgers as subsidiary accounts.

- The cash book and petty cash book should be treated as part of the double entry system unless the task instructions state otherwise.

- The VAT rate is 20%.

Task 1

Finn Clothing has started a new business, Finn Footware, and a new set of accounts is to be opened. A partially completed journal to record the opening balances is shown below.

Record the journal entries needed in the accounts in the general ledger of Finn Footware to deal with the opening balances.

Account name	Amount £	Debit ✓	Credit ✓
Capital	9,000		9,000
Cash at bank	850	850	
Furniture and fittings	1,680	1,680	
Loan from bank	4,500		4,500
Marketing expenses	300	300	
Motor expenses	90	90	
Motor van	1,150	1,150	
Purchases	8,200	8,200	
Rent and rates	510	510	
Wages	720	720	
Journal to record the opening entries of new business			

Task 2

Finn Clothing pays its employees by cheque every month and maintains a wages control account. A summary of last month's payroll transactions is shown below:

Item	£
Gross wages	10,267
Employees' NI	716
Income tax	1,540
Employer's pension contributions	150
Employer's NI	1,182

Record the journal entries needed in the general ledger to:

(a) **Record the wages expense**

Account name		Amount £	Debit ✓	Credit ✓
Wages expense	▼	11,599	✓	
Wages and salaries control	▼	11,599		✓

(b) **Record the pension administrator liability**

Account name		Amount £	Debit ✓	Credit ✓
Pension liability	▼	150		✓
WSC	▼	150	✓	

Picklist for line items:

Bank
Employees' NI
Employer's NI
HM Revenue and Customs
Income tax
Net wages
Pension administrator
Wages control
Wages expense

192

Task 3

A credit customer, Gridhaul Ltd, has ceased trading, owing Finn Clothing £760 plus VAT.

(a) **Record the journal entries needed in the general ledger to write off the net amount and the VAT.**

Account name		Amount £ ✓	Debit ✓	Credit ✓
irrecoverable debts ▾		760	✓	
VAT ▾		152	✓	
SLCA ▾		912		✓

Picklist for line items:

Irrecoverable debts
Gridhaul Ltd
Finn Clothing
Purchases
Purchases ledger control
Sales
Sales ledger control
VAT

It is important to understand the types of error that are disclosed by the trial balance and those that are not.

(b) **Show which of the errors below are, or are not, disclosed by the trial balance.**

Error in the general ledger	Error disclosed by the trial balance ✓	Error NOT disclosed by the trial balance ✓
Making a transposition error in the debit entry from the journal in the general ledger but not in the credit entry	✓	
Recording a sale to a customer for £75 cash (no VAT) as £57 in both the cash account and the sales account		✓
Recording a payment for a cash purchase (no VAT) in the trade payables column of the cash book	✓	✓
Recording discount allowed to a customer on the debit side of the discount allowed account and the debit side of the sales ledger control account	✓	
Recording a payment to a supplier on the credit side of the supplier's purchases ledger account	✓	
Recording a sales return by debiting the sales ledger control account and crediting the sales returns account		✓

One of the errors in (b) above can be classified as an error of reversal of entries.

(c) **Show which error is an error of reversal of entries.**

Error in the general ledger	✓
Making a transposition error in the debit entry from the journal in the general ledger but not in the credit entry	
Recording a sale to a customer for £75 cash (no VAT) as £57 in both the cash account and the sales account	
Recording a payment for a cash purchase (no VAT) in the trade payables column of the cash book	
Recording discount allowed to a customer on the debit side of the discount allowed account and the debit side of the sales ledger control account	
Recording a payment to a supplier on the credit side of the supplier's purchases ledger account	
Recording a sales return by debiting the sales ledger control account and crediting the sales returns account	✓

Task 4

A credit sale of £678 has been entered in the accounting records as £768. (Ignore VAT.)

(a) **Record the journal entries needed in the general ledger to remove the incorrect entry.**

Account name		Amount £	Debit ✓	Credit ✓
Sales	▼	678	✓	
SLCA	▼	678		✓

(b) Record the journal entries needed in the general ledger to record the correct entry.

Account name		Amount £	Debit ✓	Credit ✓
Sales	▼	768		✓
SLCA	▼	768	✓	

Picklist:

Bank
Cash
Sales ledger control
Trade receivables
Sales day book
Sales
Suspense

Task 5

Finn Clothing's trial balance was extracted and did not balance. The debit column of the trial balance totalled £326,537 and the credit column totalled £329,620.

(a) **What entry would be made in the suspense account to balance the trial balance?**

Account name	Amount £	Debit ✓	Credit ✓
Suspense	3083	✓	

Finn Clothing's initial trial balance includes a suspense account with a balance of £1,000.

The error has been identified as arising from an incorrectly totalled net column in the sales day book shown below.

Sales day book

Date 20XX	Details	Invoice number	Total £	VAT £	Net £
30 Jun	Idris plc	5264	1,008	168	840
30 Jun	Venitian Trading	5265	1,824	304	1,520
30 Jun	Slippers & Co	5266	2,592	432	2,160
	Totals		5,424	904	3,520

4520

(b) **Record the journal entry needed in the general ledger to remove the incorrect entry made from the sales day book.**

Account name		Amount £	Debit ✓	Credit ✓
Sales	▼	3,520	✓	

(c) **Record the journal entry needed in the general ledger to record the correct entry that should have been made from the sales day book.**

Account name		Amount £	Debit ✓	Credit ✓
Sales	▼	4520		✓

(d) **Record the journal entry needed in the general ledger to remove the suspense account balance arising from the error in the sales day book.**

Account name		Amount £	Debit ✓	Credit ✓
Su suspense	▼	1000	✓	

Picklist:

Balance b/f
Balance c/d
Net
Sales
Sales ledger control
Suspense
Trade receivables
VAT

The trial balance is an important accounting control.

(e) **Show ONE reason for producing the trial balance.**

	✓
To detect fraud	⌀
To check that double entry has been performed correctly	✓
To comply with the statutory requirement	
To save time	

Task 6

Finn Clothing's trial balance included a suspense account. All the bookkeeping errors have now been traced and the journal entries shown below have been recorded.

Journal entries

Account name	Debit £	Credit £
Suspense	3,000	
Loan		3,000
Administration expenses	265	
Irrecoverable debts		265
Purchases ledger control	174	
Suspense		174

Post the journal entries to the general ledger accounts. Dates are not required.

Administration expenses

Details	Amount £	Details	Amount £
▼		Irrecoverab.. selly ▼	265

Irrecoverable debts

Details	Amount £	Details	Amount £
A expense ▼	265	▼	

Loan

Details	Amount £	Details	Amount £
Suspense ▼	3,000	▼	

Purchases ledger control

Details	Amount £	Details	Amount £
▼		Suspense ▼	114

Suspense

Details	Amount £	Details	Amount £
PLCA ▼	114	Balance b/f	2,826
▼		loan ▼	3,000

Picklist:

Balance b/d
Administration expenses
Irrecoverable debts
Loan
Purchases ledger control
Suspense

Task 7

On 30 June Finn Clothing extracted an initial trial balance which did not balance, and a suspense account with a debit balance of £1,690 was opened. On 1 July journal entries were prepared to correct the errors that had been found, and clear the suspense account. The list of balances in the initial trial balance, and the journal entries to correct the errors, are shown below.

Journal entries

Account name	Debit £	Credit £
Furniture and fittings		8,690
Suspense	8,690	
Furniture and fittings	9,680	
Suspense		9,680

Account name	Debit £	Credit £
Sales returns	350	
Suspense		350
Sales returns	350	
Suspense		350

Taking into account the journal entries, which will clear the suspense account, re-draft the trial balance by placing the figures in the debit or credit column. Do not enter your figures with decimal places in this task and do not enter a zero in the empty column.

	Balances extracted on 30 June £	Balances at 1 July	
		Debit £	Credit £
Machinery	15,240		
Furniture and fittings	8,690		
Inventory	11,765		
Bank (overdraft)	5,127		
Petty cash	100		
Sales ledger control	72,536		
Purchases ledger control	11,928		
VAT (owing to HM Revenue and Customs)	2,094		
Capital	80,000		
Sales	98,162		
Purchases	39,278		
Purchases returns	4,120		
Wages	22,855		
Sales returns	110		
Administration expenses	10,287		
Rent and rates	12,745		
Marketing expenses	3,289		
Irrecoverable debts	1,275		
Maintenance	1,571		
Totals			

Task 8

On 25 June Finn Clothing received the following bank statement as at 23 June.

Rover Bank PLC

32 Main Square, Gridford GR3 1FP

To: Finn Clothing   Account No 33823981   23 June 20XX

Statement of Account

Date	Detail	Paid out	Paid in	Balance	
20XX		£	£	£	
04 June	Balance b/f			4,278	C
04 June	Cheque 003912	1,290		2,988	C
04 June	Cheque 003913	832		2,156	C
05 June	Cheque 003914	4,435		2,279	D
06 June	Cheque 003916	378		2,657	D
12 June	Bank Giro Credit Pebbles Sisters		3,194	537	C
13 June	Cheque 003917	1,407		870	D
13 June	Direct debit Business rates	540		1,410	D
20 June	Direct debit Insurance Inc	261		1,671	D
23 June	Bank charges	9		1,680	D
23 June	Overdraft fee	24		1,704	D
23 June	Counter credit		2,744	1,040	C

D = Debit   C = Credit

The cash book as at 23 June is shown below.

(a) **Check the items on the bank statement against the items in the cash book.**

(b) **Enter any items in the cash book as needed.**

(c) **Total the cash book and clearly show the balance carried down at 23 June (closing balance) and brought down at 24 June (opening balance).**

Cash book

Date 20XX	Details	Bank £	Date 20XX	Cheque number	Details	Bank £
01 June	Balance b/f	4,278	01 June	003912	Brisbane plc	1,290
20 June	Faulkners Finery	2,744	01 June	003913	Ventor Ltd	832
21 June	Roustabout plc	2,927	01 June	003914	Strauss Brothers	4,435
22 June	Hampleforth Ltd	456	01 June	003915	Westenholme plc	1,333
23 June	Pebbles sisters ▼	3,194	02 June	003916	Ambrosden Hunt Ltd	378
	▼		02 June	003917	Linnie Ltd	1,407
	▼		13 June	003918	Crebber plc	2,366
	▼		23 June		Insurance Co	261
	▼		23 June		Business rate ▼	540
	▼		23 June		Bank charges ▼	9
	▼		23 June		overdraft free ▼	24
	▼		23 June		Balance C/d ▼	724
	Total	13599			Total	13599
24 Jun	Balance b/d ▼	724			▼	

Picklist:

Ambrosden Hunt Ltd
Balance b/d
Balance c/d
Bank charges
Brisbane plc
Business rates
Crebber plc
Insurance Inc
Faulkners Finery

Hampleforth Ltd
Linnie Ltd
Overdraft fee
Pebbles Sisters
Roustabout plc
Strauss Brothers
Ventor Ltd
Westenholme plc

Task 9

On 25 October Finn Clothing received the following bank statement as at 23 October.

Rover Bank PLC

32 Main Square, Gridford GR3 1FP

To: Finn Clothing   Account No 33823981   23 June 20XX

Statement of Account

Date 20XX	Detail	Paid out £	Paid in £	Balance £	
01 Oct	Balance b/f			2,600	C
02 Oct	Cheque 004365	812		1,788	C
06 Oct	Cheque 004367	1,649			
06 Oct	Cheque 004366	2,548		2,409	D
14 Oct	Cheque 004370	4,613		7,022	D
17 Oct	Bank Giro Credit Hampleforth Ltd		10,000	2,978	C
18 Oct	Cheque 004368	372			
18 Oct	Bank Giro Credit Roustabout plc		1,872	4,478	C
22 Oct	Cheque 004372	1,543		2,935	C
23 Oct	Direct debit Insurance Inc	261		2,674	
23 Oct	Counter credit		2,000	4,674	C

D = Debit   C = Credit

Cash book

Date 20XX	Details	Bank £	Date 20XX	Cheque number	Details	Bank £
1 Oct	Balance b/f	1,788	1 Oct	004366	Crebber plc	2,548
17 Oct	Hampleforth Ltd	10,000	3 Oct	004367	Ambrosden Hunt Ltd	1,649
18 Oct	Roustabout plc	1,872	9 Oct	004368	Strauss Brothers	372
21 Oct	Faulkners Finery	5,468	11 Oct	004369	Ventor Ltd	3,711
23 Oct	Astley & Co (cash sale)	2,000	11 Oct	004370	Westenholme plc	4,613
23 Oct	Rent receivable	1,500	14 Oct	004371	Linnie Ltd	97
			19 Oct	004372	Brisbane plc	1,543
			23 Oct		Insurance Inc	261

(a) **Identify the FOUR transactions that are included in the cash book but missing from the bank statement and complete the bank reconciliation statement below as at 23 October.**

Bank reconciliation statement as at 23 October 20XX	£
Balance per bank statement	4,674
Add:	
Faulkners Finery ▼	5,468
Rent receivable ▼	1,500
Total to add	6,968
Less:	
Ventor Ltd ▼	3,711
Linnie Ltd ▼	97
Total to subtract	3808
Balance as per cash book	7 834

Picklist:

Ambrosden Hunt Ltd
Astley & Co
Brisbane plc
Crebber plc
Insurance Inc
Faulkners Finery
Hampleforth Ltd
Rent receivable
Linnie Ltd
Roustabout plc
Strauss Brothers
Ventor Ltd
Westenholme plc

(b) **Show whether each of the statements below is True or False.**

	True ✓	False ✓
When a customer pays Finn Clothing by cheque, the amount is credited to Finn Clothing's current account immediately it receives the cheque		✓
When it receives payment from a customer by credit card using an electronic swipe machine, an automated transfer is made into the Finn Clothing's bank current account	✓	
A customer that pays Finn Clothing by standing order makes payment of a regular amount each period	✓	

Task 10

This is a summary of transactions with suppliers during the month of June.

(a) **Show whether each entry will be a debit or credit in the purchases ledger control account in the general ledger.**

Details	Amount £	Debit ✓	Credit ✓
Balance of trade payables at 1 June	15,243		15,243
Payments made to credit suppliers	16,297	16,297	
Goods purchased on credit	17,209		17,209
Goods returned to credit suppliers	2,187	2,187	
Discount received	625	625	

(b) **What will be the balance brought down on 1 July on the above account?**

	✓
Debit £11,519	
Credit £11,519	
Debit £13,343	
Credit £13,343	
Debit £18,967	
Credit £18,967	

The following credit balances were in the purchases ledger on 1 July.

	£
Rambout plc	1,928
Creakleys	5,326
International Peace Ltd	936
Diamond Lil plc	1,278
Marksman & Co	4,425
Fitzharrys plc	327

(c) **Reconcile the balances shown above with the purchases ledger control account balance you have calculated in part (b).**

	£
Purchases ledger control account balance as at 30 June	
Total of purchases ledger accounts as at 30 June	
Difference	

(d) **What error may have caused the difference you calculated in part (c)?**

	✓
Discounts received may have been omitted from the purchases ledger	
Purchases invoices may have been entered in the purchases ledger control account twice	
Goods returned may have been entered in the purchases ledger twice	
Goods returned may have been omitted from the purchases ledger control account	

It is important to reconcile the purchases ledger control account on a regular basis.

(e) **Which of the following statements is True?**

Reconciliation of the purchases ledger control account	✓
assures managers that the amount showing as outstanding from customers is correct	
assures managers that the amount showing as outstanding to suppliers is correct	
will show if a sales invoice has been omitted from the purchases ledger	
will show if a purchases invoice has been omitted from the sales ledger	

Task 11

The following is an extract from Finn Clothing's books of prime entry.

Totals for quarter

Sales day book		Purchases day book	
Net:	£53,550	Net:	£16,275
VAT:	£10,710	VAT:	£3,255
Gross:	£64,260	Gross:	£19,530

Sales returns day book		Purchases returns day book	
Net:	£2,800	Net:	£1,085
VAT:	£560	VAT:	£217
Gross:	£3,360	Gross:	£1,302

Cash book

Net cash sales:	£840
VAT:	£168
Gross cash sales:	£1,008

(a) **What will be the entries in the VAT control account to record the VAT transactions in the quarter?**

VAT control

Details		Amount £	Details		Amount £
	▼			▼	
	▼			▼	
	▼			▼	

Picklist:

Cash book
Cash sales
Purchases
Purchases day book
Purchases returns
Purchases returns day book
Sales
Sales day book
Sales returns
Sales returns day book
VAT

The VAT return has been completed and shows an amount owing from HM Revenue and Customs of £7,280.

(b) **Is the VAT return correct?**

	✓
Yes	
No	

Task 12

(a) **From the list below identify TWO methods of automated payment.**

Service	Method of making automated payment? ✓
Cheque	
BACS	
Cash	
Standing order	
Interest	

(b) **Show whether the following statements about banking services are True or False.**

	True ✓	False ✓
No entries can be made in a cash book without access to the business's bank statement		
A mortgage is an arrangement whereby the customer can withdraw more money from the account than he has in it up to a certain limit		
A dishonoured cheque is sent back to the drawer's bank so that the drawer can pursue payment in some other way		
A cheque drawn on Bank X and paid in at Bank Y will normally take three days to be paid		
A customer with a current account at a bank will usually be able to operate it with a credit card		
In the absence of timing differences, a customer with a credit balance on its cash book must have a bank statement that shows a debit balance		

BPP PRACTICE ASSESSMENT 2
CONTROL ACCOUNTS, JOURNALS AND THE BANKING SYSTEM

ANSWERS

Control Accounts, Journals and the Banking System
BPP practice assessment 2

Task 1

Account name	Amount £	Debit ✓	Credit ✓
Capital	9,000		✓
Cash at bank	850	✓	
Furniture and fittings	1,680	✓	
Loan from bank	4,500		✓
Marketing expenses	300	✓	
Motor expenses	90	✓	
Motor van	1,150	✓	
Purchases	8,200	✓	
Rent and rates	510	✓	
Wages	720	✓	
Journal to record the opening entries of new business			

Task 2

(a)

Account name	Amount £	Debit ✓	Credit ✓
Wages expense	11,599	✓	
Wages control	11,599		✓

(b)

Account name	Amount £	Debit ✓	Credit ✓
Wages control	150	✓	
Pension administrator	150		✓

Task 3

(a)

Account name	Amount £	Debit ✓	Credit ✓
Irrecoverable debts	760	✓	
VAT	152	✓	
Sales ledger control	912		✓

(b)

Error in the general ledger	Error disclosed by the trial balance ✓	Error NOT disclosed by the trial balance ✓
Making a transposition error in the debit entry from the journal in the general ledger but not in the credit entry	✓	
Recording a sale to a customer for £75 cash (no VAT) as £57 in both the cash account and the sales account		✓
Recording a payment for a cash purchase (no VAT) in the trade payables column of the cash book		✓
Recording discount allowed to a customer on the debit side of the discount allowed account and the debit side of the sales ledger control account	✓	
Recording a payment to a supplier on the credit side of the supplier's purchases ledger account		✓
Recording a sales return by debiting the sales ledger control account and crediting the sales returns account		✓

(c)

Error in the general ledger	✓
Making a transposition error in the debit entry from the journal in the general ledger but not in the credit entry	
Recording a sale to a customer for £75 cash (no VAT) as £57 in both the cash account and the sales account	
Recording a payment for a cash purchase (no VAT) in the trade payables column of the cash book	
Recording discount allowed to a customer on the debit side of the discount allowed account and the debit side of the sales ledger control account	
Recording a payment to a supplier on the credit side of the supplier's purchases ledger account	
Recording a sales return by debiting the sales ledger control account and crediting the sales returns account	✓

Task 4

(a)

Account name	Amount £	Debit ✓	Credit ✓
Sales	768	✓	
Sales ledger control	768		✓

(b)

Account name	Amount £	Debit ✓	Credit ✓
Sales ledger control	678	✓	
Sales	678		✓

Task 5

(a)

Account name	Amount £	Debit ✓	Credit ✓
Suspense	3,083	✓	

(b)

Account name	Amount £	Debit ✓	Credit ✓
Sales	3,520	✓	

(c)

Account name	Amount £	Debit ✓	Credit ✓
Sales	4,520		✓

(d)

Account name	Amount £	Debit ✓	Credit ✓
Suspense	1,000	✓	

(e)

	✓
To detect fraud	
To check that double entry has been performed correctly	✓
To comply with the statutory requirement	
To save time	

Task 6

Administration expenses

Details	Amount £	Details	Amount £
Irrecoverable debts	265		

Irrecoverable debts

Details	Amount £	Details	Amount £
		Administration expenses	265

Loan

Details	Amount £	Details	Amount £
		Suspense	3,000

Purchases ledger control

Details	Amount £	Details	Amount £
Suspense	174		

Suspense

Details	Amount £	Details	Amount £
Loan	3,000	Balance b/f	2,826
		Purchases ledger control	174

Task 7

	Balances extracted on 30 June £	Balances at 1 July	
		Debit £	Credit £
Machinery	15,240	15,240	
Furniture and fittings	8,690	9,680	
Inventory	11,765	11,765	
Bank (overdraft)	5,127		5,127
Petty cash	100	100	
Sales ledger control	72,536	72,536	
Purchases ledger control	11,928		11,928
VAT (owing to HM Revenue and Customs)	2,094		2,094
Capital	80,000		80,000
Sales	98,162		98,162
Purchases	39,278	39,278	
Purchases returns	4,120		4,120
Wages	22,855	22,855	
Sales returns	110	810	
Administration expenses	10,287	10,287	
Rent and rates	12,745	12,745	
Marketing expenses	3,289	3,289	
Irrecoverable debts	1,275	1,275	
Maintenance	1,571	1,571	
	Totals	201,431	201,431

Task 8

(a) – (c)

Cash book

Date 20XX	Details	Bank £	Date 20XX	Cheque number	Details	Bank £
01 June	Balance b/f	4,278	01 June	003912	Brisbane plc	1,290
20 June	Faulkners Finery	2,744	01 June	003913	Ventor Ltd	832
21 June	Roustabout plc	2,927	01 June	003914	Strauss Brothers	4,435
22 June	Hampleforth Ltd	456	01 June	003915	Westenholme plc	1,333
12 June	Pebbles Sisters	3,194	02 June	003916	Ambrosden Hunt Ltd	378
			02 June	003917	Linnie Ltd	1,407
			13 June	003918	Crebber plc	2,366
			23 June		Insurance Inc	261
			13 June		Business rates	540
			23 June		Bank charges	9
			23 June		Overdraft fee	24
			23 June		Balance c/d	724
	Total	13,599			Total	13,599
24 June	Balance b/d	724				

Task 9

(a)

Bank reconciliation statement as at 23 October 20XX	£
Balance per bank statement	4,674
Add:	
Faulkners Finery	5,468
Rent receivable	1,500
Total to add	6,968
Less:	
Ventor Ltd	3,711
Linnie Ltd	97
Total to subtract	3,808
Balance as per cash book	7,834

(b)

	True ✓	False ✓
When a customer pays Finn Clothing by cheque, the amount is credited to Finn Clothing's current account immediately it receives the cheque		✓
When it receives payment from a customer by credit card using an electronic swipe machine, an automated transfer is made into the Finn Clothing's bank current account	✓	
A customer that pays Finn Clothing by standing order makes payment of a regular amount each period	✓	

Task 10

(a)

Details	Amount £	Debit ✓	Credit ✓
Balance of trade payables at 1 June	15,243		✓
Payments made to credit suppliers	16,297	✓	
Goods purchased on credit	17,209		✓
Goods returned to credit suppliers	2,187	✓	
Discount received	625	✓	

(b) The correct answer is: Credit £13,343

(c)

	£
Purchases ledger control account balance as at 30 June	13,343
Total of purchases ledger accounts as at 30 June	14,220
Difference	877

(d) The correct answer is: Discounts received may have been omitted from the purchases ledger

(e) The correct answer is: assures managers that the amount showing as outstanding to suppliers is correct

Task 11

(a)

VAT control

Details	Amount £	Details	Amount £
Sales returns	560	Sales	10,710
Purchases	3,255	Purchases returns	217
		Cash sales	168

(b) The correct answer is: No

The account has a credit balance of £7,280, that is the business owes HMRC £7,280

Task 12

(a) The correct answers are: BACS and Standing order

(b)

	True ✓	False ✓
No entries can be made in a cash book without access to the business's bank statement		✓
A mortgage is an arrangement whereby the customer can withdraw more money from the account than he has in it up to a certain limit		✓
A dishonoured cheque is sent back to the drawer's bank so that the drawer can pursue payment in some other way		✓
A cheque drawn on Bank X and paid in at Bank Y will normally take three days to be paid	✓	
A customer with a current account at a bank will usually be able to operate it with a credit card		✓
In the absence of timing differences, a customer with a credit balance on its cash book must have a bank statement that shows a debit balance	✓	

BPP PRACTICE ASSESSMENT 3
CONTROL ACCOUNTS, JOURNALS AND THE BANKING SYSTEM

Time allowed: 2 hours

PRACTICE ASSESSMENT 3

Control Accounts, Journals and the Banking System
BPP practice assessment 3

- You are employed by the business, Scriven Trading, as a bookkeeper.

- Scriven Trading uses a manual accounting system.

- Double entry takes place in the general ledger. Individual accounts of trade receivables and trade payables are kept in the sales and purchases ledgers as subsidiary accounts.

- The cash book and petty cash book should be treated as part of the double entry system unless the task instructions state otherwise.

- The VAT rate is 20%.

Task 1

Scriven Trading has started a new business, Scriven Supplies, and a new set of accounts is to be opened. A partially completed journal to record the opening balances is shown below.

Record the journal entries needed in the accounts in the general ledger of Scriven Supplies to deal with the opening balances.

Account name	Amount £	Debit ✓	Credit ✓
Capital	14,560		14,560
Bank overdraft	2,380		2,380
Computer equipment	12,840	12,840	
Loan from bank	8,100		8100
Administration expenses	790	790	
Travel expenses	330	330	
Machinery	9,800	9800	
Purchases	3,250	3250	
Sales	2,370		2,370
Wages	400	400	
Journal to record the opening entries of new business			

Task 2

Scriven Trading pays its employees by cheque every month and maintains a wages control account. A summary of last month's payroll transactions is shown below:

Item	£
Gross wages	15,409
Employees' NI	781
Income tax	1,673
Employees' social club contributions	150
Employer's NI	2,390

(a) **Show the journal entries needed in the general ledger to record the HM Revenue and Customs liability.**

Account name	Amount £	Debit ✓	Credit ✓
HMRC ▼	4844		✓
Wages control ▼	4844	✓	

(b) **Show the journal entries needed in the general ledger to record the social club administrator liability.**

Account name	Amount £	Debit ✓	Credit ✓
Social club administrator ▼	150		✓
Wages control ▼	150	✓	

Picklist:

Bank
Employees' NI
Employer's NI
HM Revenue and Customs
Income tax
Net wages
Social club administrator
Wages control
Wages expense

Task 3

A credit customer, Havelock Co, has ceased trading, owing Scriven Trading £1,560 including VAT.

(a) **Record the journal entries needed in the general ledger to write off the net amount and the VAT.**

Account name		Amount £	Debit ✓	Credit ✓
Irrecoverable debts ▼		1300	✓	
VAT ▼		260	✓	
SLCR ▼		1560		✓

Picklist:

Havelock Co
Irrecoverable debts
Purchases
Purchases ledger control
Sales
Sales ledger control
Scriven Trading
VAT

It is important to understand the types of error that are disclosed by the trial balance and those that are not.

(b) **Show which of the errors below are, or are not, disclosed by the trial balance.**

Error in the general ledger	Error disclosed by the trial balance ✓	Error NOT disclosed by the trial balance ✓
For a cash sale of £340 (no VAT), recording the amount as £34 in the cash book		✓
Recording £50 discount received on the credit side of PLCA and the debit side of the discount received account		✓
Recording a purchase from a supplier for £180 including VAT as £180 in the PLCA and purchases accounts and £30 in the VAT account	✓	
Making a transposition error when transferring a balance from the ledger account to the trial balance	✓	
Recording a payment from a credit customer for £200 in the debit side of the sales ledger account	✓	
Making a casting error in the total column of the sales returns day book	✓	

One of the errors in (b) above can be classified as a balance transfer error.

(c) **Show which error is a balance transfer error.**

Error in the general ledger	✓
For a cash sale of £340 (no VAT), recording the amount as £34 in the cash book	
Recording £50 discount received on the credit side of PLCA and the debit side of the discount received account	
Recording a purchase from a supplier for £180 including VAT as £180 in the PLCA and purchases accounts and £30 in the VAT account	
Making a transposition error when transferring a balance from the ledger account to the trial balance	✓
Recording a payment from a credit customer for £200 in the debit side of the sales ledger account	
Making a casting error in the total column of the sales returns day book	

Task 4

A credit purchase return of £1,170 has been entered in the accounting records as £1,710. (Ignore VAT.)

(a) **Record the journal entries needed in the general ledger to remove the incorrect entry.**

Account name	Amount £	Debit ✓	Credit ✓
purchase return	1,710	✓	
plcpuse	1,710		✓

(b) **Record the journal entries needed in the general ledger to record the correct entry.**

Account name	Amount £	Debit ✓	Credit ✓
purchase returns	1170		✓
plca	1170	✓	

Picklist:

Bank
Cash
Purchases ledger control
Purchases returns day book
Purchases returns
Suspense
Trade payables

Task 5

Scriven Trading's trial balance was extracted and did not balance. The debit column of the trial balance totalled £401,845 and the credit column totalled £398,206.

(a) **What entry would be made in the suspense account to balance the trial balance?**

Account name	Amount £	Debit ✓	Credit ✓
Suspense	3639		✓

In the following month Scriven Trading's initial trial balance includes a suspense account with a balance of £63.

The error has now been identified as arising from an incorrectly totalled VAT column in the sales returns day book shown below.

Sales returns day book

Date 20XX	Details	Credit note number	Total £	VAT £	Net £
30 Jun	Humber Ltd	201	3,396	566	2,830
30 Jun	Stomes Co	202	1,848	308	1,540
30 Jun	Carswell Brothers	203	864	144	720
	Totals		6,108	1,081	5,090

(b) **Record the journal entry needed in the general ledger to remove the incorrect entry made from the sales returns day book.**

Account name	Amount £	Debit ✓	Credit ✓
Sales VAT returns	1081		✓

(c) **Record the journal entry needed in the general ledger to record the correct entry that should have been made from the sales returns day book.**

Account name		Amount £	Debit ✓	Credit ✓
~~Sales~~ VAT Control ▼		1 018	✓	

(d) **Record the journal entry needed in the general ledger to remove the suspense account balance arising from the error in the sales returns day book.**

Account name		Amount £	Debit ✓	Credit ✓
Suspense ▼		63	✓	✓

Picklist:

Balance b/f
Balance c/d
Sales
Sales returns
Suspense
Total
Trade receivables
VAT

The entry to record a receipt from a credit customer of £2,309 has been recorded as £2,930 in the sales ledger.

(e) **Complete the following statement.**

As a result of this error, the customer's balance will be

	✓
Too high	
Too low	✓

Task 6

Scriven Trading's trial balance included a suspense account. All the bookkeeping errors have now been traced and the journal entries shown below have been recorded.

Journal entries

Account name	Debit £	Credit £
Sales ledger control	205	
Suspense		205
Irrecoverable debts	189	
Suspense		189
Motor vehicles	3,300	
Machinery		3,300

Post the journal entries to the general ledger accounts.

Irrecoverable debts

Details		Amount £	Details		Amount £
Suspense	▼	189		▼	
	▼			▼	
	▼			▼	

Machinery

Details		Amount £	Details		Amount £
	▼		Motor vehicles	▼	3,300
	▼			▼	
	▼			▼	

Motor vehicles

Details		Amount £	Details		Amount £
Machinery	▼	3300		▼	
	▼			▼	
	▼			▼	

Sales ledger control

Details		Amount £	Details		Amount £
Suspense	▼	205		▼	
	▼			▼	
	▼			▼	

Suspense

Details		Amount £	Details		Amount £
Balance b/f		394	SLCA	▼	205
SLCA	▼	205	Irrecovrable debts	▼	189
	▼			▼	

Picklist for line items:

Balance b/d
Irrecoverable debts
Machinery
Motor vehicles
Sales ledger control
Suspense

- -

Task 7

On 30 June Scriven Trading extracted an initial trial balance which did not balance, and a suspense account was opened with a £2,660 debit balance. On 1 July journal entries were prepared to correct the errors that had been found, and clear the suspense account. The list of balances in the initial trial balance, and the journal entries to correct the errors, are shown below.

Journal entries

Account name	Debit £	Credit £
Purchases ledger control	9,820	
Suspense		9,820
Purchases ledger control		9,280
Suspense	9,280	

Account name	Debit £	Credit £
Office expenses	1,060	
Suspense		1,060
Office expenses	1,060	
Suspense		1,060

Taking into account the journal entries, which will clear the suspense account, re-draft the trial balance by placing the figures in the debit or credit column. Do not enter your figures with decimal places in this task and do not enter a zero in the empty column.

	Balances extracted on 30 June £	Balances at 1 July	
		Debit £	Credit £
Motor vehicles	12,300	12,300	
Machinery	17,650	17,650	
Inventory	4,380	4,380	
Cash at bank	1,470	1470	
Petty cash	150	150	
Sales ledger control	43,330	43,330	
Purchases ledger control	9,820	8	9,280
VAT (owing to HM Revenue and Customs)	2,660		2,660
Capital	25,000		25,000
Sales	173,200		173,200
Purchases	79,610	79,610	
Purchases returns	1,640		1640
Wages	40,650	40650	
Sales returns	2,170	2170	
Office expenses	1,260	3380	
Bank loan	14,390		14,390
Production expenses	16,240	16240	
Irrecoverable debts	2,880	2,880	
Travel expenses	1,960	1960	
Totals		226170	226170

Task 8

On 28 June Scriven Trading received the following bank statement as at 23 June.

Strongs Bank PLC

14-18 High Street, Handtown HA3 9XC

To: Scriven Trading   Account No 11115627   23 June 20XX

Statement of Account

Date 20XX	Detail	Paid out £	Paid in £	Balance £	
04 June	Balance b/f			1,629	C
04 June	Cheque 112341	782		847	C
04 June	Cheque 112342	1,435		588	D
05 June	Cheque 112343	5,003		5,591	D
06 June	Cheque 112345	909		6,500	D
12 June	Bank Giro Credit Longwall Co		8,014	1,514	C
13 June	Cheque 112346	2,387		873	D
13 June	Direct debit Business rates	470		1,343	D
20 June	Direct debit Trio Rentals	650		1,993	D
23 June	Bank charges (1)	15		2,008	D
23 June	Bank charges (2)	61		2,069	D
23 June	Counter credit		5,839	3,770	C

D = Debit   C = Credit

(a) **Check the items on the bank statement against the items in the cash book.**

(b) **Enter any items in the cash book as needed.**

(c) **Total the cash book and clearly show the balance carried down at 23 June and brought down at 24 June.**

Cash book

Date 20XX	Details	Bank £	Date 20XX	Cheque number	Details	Bank £
01 June	Balance b/f	1,629	01 June	112341	Fieldens & Co	782
20 June	Esterholme plc	5,839	01 June	112342	Quisdem plc	1,435
21 June	Moben Triss	3,279	01 June	112343	Pressway and Sons	5,003
22 June	Stoney Crane	1,207	01 June	112344	Kibble Co	3,226
	▼		02 June	112345	Nimble Partners	909
	▼		02 June	112346	Folly Bridge Ltd	2,387
	▼		13 June	112347	Fosdyke Ltd	846
	▼		20 June		Trio Rentals	650
	▼				▼	
	▼				▼	
	▼				▼	
	▼				▼	
	Total				Total	
	▼				▼	

Picklist:

Balance b/d
Balance c/d
Bank charges (1)
Bank charges (2)
Business rates
Esterholme plc
Fieldens & Co
Folly Bridge Ltd
Fosdyke Ltd
Kibble Co
Longwall Co
Moben Triss
Nimble Partners
Pressway and Sons
Quisdem plc
Stoney Crane
Trio Rentals

Task 9

(a) On 26 September Scriven Trading received the following bank statement as at 23 September.

Strongs Bank PLC

14-18 High Street, Handtown HA3 9XC

To: Scriven Trading   Account No 11115627   23 September 20XX

Statement of Account

Date	Detail	Paid out	Paid in	Balance
20XX		£	£	£
04 Sept	Balance b/f			2,987
07 Sept	Cheque 115046	1,897		1,090
09 Sept	Cheque 115047	2,681		1,591
10 Sept	Bank Giro Credit Esterholme plc		789	802
16 Sept	Counter credit		4,293	3,491
18 Sept	Cheque 115050	3,125		366
19 Sept	Cheque 115048	2,224		1,858
21 Sept	Cheque 115051	95		1,953
20 Sept	Direct debit Trio Rentals	650		2,603

D = Debit   C = Credit

Cash book

Date 20XX	Details	Bank £	Date 20XX	Cheque number	Details	Bank £
4 Sept	Balance b/f	2,987	4 Sept	115046	Kibble Co	1,897
9 Sept	Esterholme plc	789	6 Sept	115047	Fosdyke Ltd	2,681
16 Sept	Moben Triss	1,651	11 Sept	115048	Folly Bridge Ltd	2,224
16 Sept	Stoney Crane	2,642	12 Sept	115049	Fieldens & Co	1,643
21 Sept	Urquhart plc	4,647	15 Sept	115050	Nimble Partners	3,125
23 Sept	Rathbones	3,225	18 Sept	115051	Pressway and Sons	95
			20 Sept		Trio Rentals	650
			22 Sept	115052	Quisdem plc	456

Identify the FOUR transactions that are included in the cash book but missing from the bank statement and complete the bank reconciliation statement below as at 23 September.

Bank reconciliation statement as at 23 September 20XX	£
Balance per bank statement	
Add:	
▼	
▼	
Total to add	
Less:	
▼	
▼	
Total to subtract	
Balance as per cash book	

Picklist:

Balance b/d
Balance c/d
Esterholme plc
Fieldens & Co
Folly Bridge Ltd
Fosdyke Ltd
Kibble Co
Moben Triss
Nimble Partners
Pressway and Sons
Quisdem plc
Rathbones
Stoney Crane
Trio Rentals
Urquhart plc

(b) **Show whether each of the statements below is True or False.**

	True ✓	False ✓
When a customer pays Scriven Trading by cheque, the amount is not usually available to Scriven Trading immediately	✓	
A customer's credit card payment processed using an online card machine means that Scriven Trading receives the funds on the day of the transaction	✓	
If Scriven Trading wishes to pay irregular amounts at regular times to a supplier it should use a standing order		✓

Task 10

This is a summary of transactions with customers during the month of June.

(a) **Show whether each entry will be a debit or credit in the sales ledger control account in the general ledger.**

Details	Amount £	Debit ✓	Credit ✓
Balance of trade receivables at 1 June	13,289	13,289	
Payments received from credit customers	14,911		14,911
Goods sold on credit	16,435	16,435	
Goods returned by credit customers	1,452		1,452
Discount allowed	43		43

(b) **What will be the balance brought down on 1 July on the above account?**

	✓
Debit £16,222	
Credit £16,222	
Debit £13,404	
Credit £13,404	
Debit £13,318	✓
Credit £13,318	

The following debit balances were in the sales ledger on 1 July.

	£
Sistema plc	2,826
Pardew and Sons	983
Lascelles plc	1,330
Gimsters Co	762
Jerowby Fine	5,111
Masonry Parks	2,360

(c) **Reconcile the balances shown above with the sales ledger control account balance you have calculated in part (b).**

	£
Sales ledger control account balance as at 30 June	13,318
Total of sales ledger accounts as at 30 June	13 372
Difference	54

(d) **What error may have caused the difference you calculated in part (c)?**

	✓
Discounts allowed may have been omitted from the control account	
A transposition error in entering an invoice in the sales day book	
An irrecoverable debt write-off omitted from the sales ledger	✓
A credit note entered twice in the sales ledger	

It is important to reconcile the sales ledger control account on a regular basis.

(e) **Which of the following statements is True?**

Reconciliation of the sales ledger control account	✓
assures managers that the amount showing as cash at bank is correct	
assures managers that the amount showing as outstanding to suppliers is correct	
will show if a sales invoice has been omitted from the sales ledger	✓
will show if a payment has been omitted from the purchases ledger	

Task 11

The following is an extract from Scriven Trading's books of prime entry.

Totals for quarter

Sales day book		**Purchases day book**	
Net:	£21,430	Net:	£11,720
VAT:	£4,286	VAT:	£2,344
Gross:	£25,716	Gross:	£14,064

Sales returns day book		**Purchases returns day book**	
Net:	£1,260	Net:	£970
VAT:	£252	VAT:	£194
Gross:	£1,512	Gross:	£1,164

Cash book

Net cash sales:	£1,350
VAT:	£270
Gross cash sales:	£1,620

(a) **What will be the entries in the VAT control account to record the VAT transactions in the quarter?**

VAT control

Details		Amount £	Details		Amount £
Purchase	▼	2344	Sales	▼	4286
Sales returns	▼	252	Purchase returns	▼	194
	▼		Cash book	▼	270

Picklist:

Cash book
Cash sales
Purchases
Purchases day book
Purchases returns
Purchases returns day book
Sales
Sales day book
Sales returns
Sales returns day book
VAT

The VAT return has been completed and shows an amount owing to HM Revenue and Customs of £1,641.

(b) **Is the VAT return correct?**

	✓
Yes	
No	✓

Task 12

(a) **From the list below identify TWO methods of automated payment.**

Service	Method of making automated payment? ✓
CHAPS	✓
Cheque	
Bank draft	
Cash	
BACS	✓

(b) **Show whether the following statements about banking services are True or False.**

	True ✓	False ✓
A bank's nightsafe allows customers to withdraw cash whenever they wish		✓
The 'account payee' crossing on a cheque means that it must only be paid into a bank account in the payee's name	✓	
On a bank statement, an overdrawn balance is called a credit balance		✓
The banking system for debit card payments means they are taken out of the bank account after three days		✓
A bank will charge its customer a fee for making a CHAPS payment	✓	
A bank is entitled to debit its customer's overdrawn account with interest due	✓	

BPP PRACTICE ASSESSMENT 3 CONTROL ACCOUNTS, JOURNALS AND THE BANKING SYSTEM

ANSWERS

Control Accounts, Journals and the Banking System
BPP practice assessment 3

Task 1

Account name	Amount £	Debit ✓	Credit ✓
Capital	14,560		14,560
Bank overdraft	2,380		2,380
Computer equipment	12,840	12,840	
Loan from bank	8,100		8,100
Administration expenses	790	790	
Travel expenses	330	330	
Machinery	9,800	9,800	
Purchases	3,250	3,250	
Sales	2,370		2,370
Wages	400	400	
Journal to record the opening entries of new business			

Task 2

(a)

Account name	Amount £	Debit ✓	Credit ✓
Wages control	4,844	✓	
HM Revenue and Customs	4,844		✓

(b)

Account name	Amount £	Debit ✓	Credit ✓
Wages control	150	✓	
Social club administrator	150		✓

Task 3

(a)

Account name	Amount £	Debit ✓	Credit ✓
Irrecoverable debts	1,300	✓	
VAT	260	✓	
Sales ledger control	1,560		✓

(b)

Error in the general ledger	Error disclosed by the trial balance ✓	Error NOT disclosed by the trial balance ✓
For a cash sale of £340 (no VAT), recording the amount as £34 in the cash book		✓
Recording £50 discount received on the credit side of PLCA and the debit side of the discount received account		✓
Recording a purchase from a supplier for £180 including VAT as £180 in the PLCA and purchases accounts and £30 in the VAT account	✓	
Making a transposition error when transferring a balance from the ledger account to the trial balance	✓	
Recording a payment from a credit customer for £200 in the debit side of the sales ledger account		✓
Making a casting error in the total column of the sales returns day book	✓	

(c)

Error in the general ledger	✓
For a cash sale of £340 (no VAT), recording the amount as £34 in the cash book	
Recording £50 discount received on the credit side of PLCA and the debit side of the discount received account	
Recording a purchase from a supplier for £180 including VAT as £180 in the PLCA and purchases accounts and £30 in the VAT account	
Making a transposition error when transferring a balance from the ledger account to the trial balance	✓
Recording a payment from a credit customer for £200 in the debit side of the sales ledger account	
Making a casting error in the total column of the sales returns day book	

Task 4

(a)

Account name	Amount £	Debit ✓	Credit ✓
Purchases returns	1,710	✓	
Purchases ledger control	1,710		✓

(b)

Account name	Amount £	Debit ✓	Credit ✓
Purchases ledger control	1,170	✓	
Purchases returns	1,170		✓

Task 5

(a)

Account name	Amount £	Debit ✓	Credit ✓
Suspense	3,639		✓

(b)

Account name	Amount £	Debit ✓	Credit ✓
VAT	1,081		✓

(c)

Account name	Amount £	Debit ✓	Credit ✓
VAT	1,018	✓	

(d)

Account name	Amount £	Debit ✓	Credit ✓
Suspense	63	✓	

(e)

As a result of this error, the customer's balance will be

	✓
Too high	
Too low	✓

Task 6

Irrecoverable debts

Details	Amount £	Details	Amount £
Suspense	189		

Machinery

Details	Amount £	Details	Amount £
		Motor vehicles	3,300

Motor vehicles

Details	Amount £	Details	Amount £
Machinery	3,300		

Sales ledger control

Details	Amount £	Details	Amount £
Suspense	205		

Suspense

Details	Amount £	Details	Amount £
Balance b/f	394	Irrecoverable debts	189
		Sales ledger control	205

Task 7

	Balances extracted on 30 June £	Balances at 1 July	
		Debit £	Credit £
Motor vehicles	12,300	12,300	
Machinery	17,650	17,650	
Inventory	4,380	4,380	
Cash at bank	1,470	1,470	
Petty cash	150	150	
Sales ledger control	43,330	43,330	
Purchases ledger control	9,820		9,280
VAT (owing to HM Revenue and Customs)	2,660		2,660
Capital	25,000		25,000
Sales	173,200		173,200
Purchases	79,610	79,610	
Purchases returns	1,640		1,640
Wages	40,650	40,650	
Sales returns	2,170	2,170	
Office expenses	1,260	3,380	
Bank loan	14,390		14,390
Production expenses	16,240	16,240	
Irrecoverable debts	2,880	2,880	
Travel expenses	1,960	1,960	
Totals		226,170	226,170

Task 8

(a) – (c)

Cash book

Date 20XX	Details	Bank £	Date 20XX	Cheque number	Details	Bank £
01 June	Balance b/f	1,629	01 June	112341	Fieldens & Co	782
20 June	Esterholme plc	5,839	01 June	112342	Quisdem plc	1,435
21 June	Moben Triss	3,279	01 June	112343	Pressway and Sons	5,003
22 June	Stoney Crane	1,207	01 June	112344	Kibble Co	3,226
12 June	Longwall Co	8,014	02 June	112345	Nimble Partners	909
			02 June	112346	Folly Bridge Ltd	2,387
			13 June	112347	Fosdyke Ltd	846
			20 June		Trio Rentals	650
			13 June		Business rates	470
			23 June		Bank charges (1)	15
			23 June		Bank charges (2)	61
			23 June		Balance c/d	4,184
	Total	19,968			Total	19,968
24 June	Balance b/d	4,184				

Task 9

(a)

Bank reconciliation statement as at 23 September 20XX	£
Balance per bank statement	−2,603
Add:	
Urquhart plc	4,647
Rathbones	3,225
Total to add	7,872
Less:	
Fieldens & Co	1,643
Quisdem plc	456
Total to subtract	2,099
Balance as per cash book	3,170

Tutorial note: the amount paid in on 16 September is made up of the two amounts, from Moben Triss and Stoney Crane, in the cash book on that day.

(b)

	True ✓	False ✓
When a customer pays Scriven Trading by cheque, the amount is not usually available to Scriven Trading immediately	✓	
A customer's credit card payment processed using an online card machine means that Scriven Trading receives the funds on the day of the transaction	✓	
If Scriven Trading wishes to pay irregular amounts at regular times to a supplier it should use a standing order		✓

Task 10

(a)

Details	Amount £	Debit ✓	Credit ✓
Balance of trade receivables at 1 June	13,289	✓	
Payments received from credit customers	14,911		✓
Goods sold on credit	16,435	✓	
Goods returned by credit customers	1,452		✓
Discount allowed	43		✓

(b)   The correct answer is: Debit £13,318

(c)

	£
Sales ledger control account balance as at 30 June	13,318
Total of sales ledger accounts as at 30 June	13,372
Difference	54

(d)   The correct answer is: An irrecoverable debt write-off omitted from the sales ledger

(e)   The correct answer is: will show if a sales invoice has been omitted from the sales ledger

Task 11

(a)

VAT control

Details	Amount £	Details	Amount £
Purchases	2,344	Sales	4,286
Sales returns	252	Purchases returns	194
		Cash sales	270

(b)   The correct answer is: No

Task 12

(a)   The correct answers are: CHAPS and BACS

(b)

	True ✓	False ✓
A bank's nightsafe allows customers to withdraw cash whenever they wish		✓
The 'account payee' crossing on a cheque means that it must only be paid into a bank account in the payee's name	✓	
On a bank statement, an overdrawn balance is called a credit balance		✓
The banking system for debit card payments means they are taken out of the bank account after three days		✓
A bank will charge its customer a fee for making a CHAPS payment	✓	
A bank is entitled to debit its customer's overdrawn account with interest due	✓	

Notes

Notes

Notes

Notes

Notes